D0090315

EXECUTIVE
ESP

EXECUTIVE
E S P

ACCESS YOUR INTUITION
FOR BUSINESS SUCCESS

GERALD JACKSON

POCKET BOOKS
New York   London   Toronto   Sydney   Tokyo

An *Original* Publication of POCKET BOOKS

 POCKET BOOKS, a division of Simon & Schuster Inc.
1230 Avenue of the Americas, New York, NY 10020

ISBN: 0-671-66748-3

First Pocket Books trade hardcover printing June 1989

10 9 8 7 6 5 4 3 2 1

POCKET and colophon are trademarks of
Simon & Schuster Inc.

Printed in the U.S.A.

FOR Judy

Acknowledgments

Many heartfelt thanks to Connie Church, for being my guardian angel; Jack Romanos, president of Pocket Books, for suggesting I do this book; Claire Zion, for her brilliant insights and sharp editorial skills; and Roderick Townley, for lending his time, talent, and energy to this project.

I would also like to thank my family and dear friends for their love and support throughout my career.

And finally, many blessings to my clients for sharing their experiences with me and for their trust in my work.

Contents

9

CONTENTS

THREE

Managing People Through Intuition

Preface

For the past twelve years I have been a professional clairvoyant, intuitive counselor, and astrologer. During that time I have helped thousands of people sort out their personal and professional problems. Some are people you may never dream would consult a psychic, like your next-door neighbor; others have been luminaries in the world of entertainment, government, and high finance.

My work has been profiled in *Financial World, Newsday,* ABC's "Eyewitness News," and hundreds of other newspapers, magazines, television and radio broadcasts. I have written this book to help you learn to use the tools I use everyday in my work, because I believe everyone has the potential to develop their intuitive nature for succeeding in life. This book has a very practical slant—how to use your intuition for business success—because the workplace is where I believe the proof of psychic ability will ultimately be accepted by the American public. It is my intention in condensing my lectures and seminars into a readily accessible programmed text to take psychic work out of the laboratories, séance parlors, and sideshow gypsy tents, and bring it into the mainstream where it belongs, free of the fear, ridicule, and misinformation it has been subject to in the past.

11

PREFACE

Many people will privately admit their belief in psychic phenomena, but few will publicly acknowledge it for fear of ridicule. I believe the skills taught in *Executive ESP: Access Your Intuition for Business Success* will be used as a textbook in the business schools of the 1990s. It is time to take the New Age out of the closet and put its practical principles to work for you, now.

Gerald Jackson

EXECUTIVE

ESP

Introduction

We've all had them: the gut feeling, the hunch, the sixth sense, the instinct, the nagging feeling, the vague intuition. Somehow you just *know* that a certain new marketing technique will succeed, that a certain investment opportunity will pay off, that a new account executive is just not going to work out, despite his sterling résumé. Frequently, the rational mind jumps in to persuade you to ignore your hunch, arguing that such twitches of intuition are not reliable, and anyway, what are they? Where do they come from? Surely you don't want to make important business decisions on the basis of a whim.

If you do stick by your instinct, and it turns out you were right, the feeling of vindication may be as heady as your sense of surprise. You ask yourself, Did I just get lucky, or is there really such a thing as a sixth sense?

If you've ignored your instinct, on the other hand, choosing to stay with conventional business approaches, you may end up kicking yourself. Few people kick themselves harder than those who just *knew* what they should have done and didn't do it.

"There were lots of little red flags that I didn't pay enough attention to," says Al Frank, who writes the *Prudent Speculator,* an investment newsletter. "I'm really disgusted with

15

myself." Because Frank ignored those promptings of information and instinct, he failed to advise his clients to bail out of the stock market in the weeks preceding Black Monday, October 19th, 1987, when the Dow plummeted 508 points. He wasn't alone. Almost all of the big investment newsletters failed to warn their readers of the impending crash.

Among the very few analysts who did warn their clients were people willing to go beyond conventional ways of thinking. One of them is Mason Sexton, whose wave theory of market activity depends as much on astrology as on computer projections. Two weeks before the crash, he warned: "Any Dow close below 2387 would be a signal to sell all stocks." He took his own advice and sold, saving himself and his clients a great deal of money.

In the hard-headed world of Wall Street, you'd think that anyone talking about astrology would be laughed off the Street, as would someone who admitted that he based his decisions on intuition. But the truth is, successful men and women throughout history have always made end runs around mere rational thinking. Julius Caesar listened to the sibyls; J. P. Morgan consulted the psychic Evangeline Adams; and in the present-day business world Conrad Hilton is said to rely on intuition to help him decide what prices to bid for properties. Many high-level executives, in fact, put off major decisions until they've had a talk with their psychic.

Former President Reagan and his wife Nancy provide one of the most famous recent examples of high-powered people who've used nontraditional methods of information-gathering. They would consult regularly with astrologer Joan Quigley about the best time to schedule presidential activities, especially anything involving travel. All sorts of events, from the timing of vacations to the signing of international agreements, were affected by the astrological advice the Reagans received.

The public mind may still harbor a great deal of skepticism about astrology, but there is much less stigma attached to the idea of intuition. As a matter of fact, many of today's executives are themselves intuitive. "More than 80 percent of CEOs who had doubled their company's profits within a five-year period," writes Roy Rowan in *The Intuitive Manager,* "proved to have above-average precognitive powers."

I can tell you, as a psychic with more than twelve years' experience advising corporations, executives, and Wall Street brokers, that the power of "direct cognition" does exist and can be taught. It is inherent in all of us, although usually undeveloped. It's called extrasensory perception, or ESP, and like musical ability it appears much more strongly in some people than in others.

Carefully controlled experiments, such as those conducted over many years at the Institute of Parapsychology by Duke University professor J. B. Rhine and others, have documented the existence of extrasensory perception beyond a reasonable doubt. Other important research has been conducted by the Mobius Society, the McDonnell Laboratory, SRI International, and the Institute of Noetic Sciences. Some researchers believe the pineal gland is the seat of extrasensory ability, although there is plenty of controversy about this. Some conjecture that ESP is related to quantum mechanics and unified field theory, although physicists such as Stephen Hawking reject that notion. There is also controversy about whether intuition is a physical or a spiritual power, or a combination of the two.

We'll leave the controversies to others. The point of this book is to help you, the adventurous executive, educate your hunches and increase the accuracy and frequency of your intuitions.

The idea is not to develop intuition to the exclusion of logical thinking, but to use these abilities in conjunction with each other. It's analogous to the functions of the right and left hemispheres of the brain; each controls different abilities, yet both sides are necessary to the fully expressed human being. The left side seems to play a dominant role in linguistic ability and logical thinking processes, whereas the right side has more to do with spatial perception, emotions, and intuition.

These are all precious human faculties, skills that can be developed, yet in our business and financial dealings the intuitive part of us is frequently disparaged, and perhaps feared, because it is irrational.

17

Such an attitude constitutes, in business terms, a great underutilization of resources. To illustrate how divided people tend to be, and to see where you currently stand, compare the following lists. In which column do you feel most comfortable?

logic	intuition
work	play
mathematics	music
research	contemplation
analysis	dream
sun	moon
history	poetry
objective	subjective
sequence	simultaneity
line	field
Western	Eastern
argument	prayer

Probably, most executives will find themselves at home with the list on the left; it is the language they speak every day. In a real sense, this book is a language course, training you to speak the forgotten language of the sub- or super-conscious. It is a language of images and associations, rather than of straight, up-and-down logic. It is the sudden grasping of a pattern, rather than the laborious following of a sequence. It involves lateral, rather than vertical, thought.

Of course, to assign the words in the left-hand column to the left hemisphere of the brain and the words on the right to the right hemisphere would be an oversimplification. Some careless or overenthusiastic theorists have done just that, making it seem that the two hemispheres are in opposition, when in fact they work in cooperation and share many functions. The two lists, then, represent a metaphorical image of two modes of consciousness, rather than a strictly scientific description of brain function.

The same is true of discussions of alpha and beta brain waves. Practical problem-solving tends to be associated with fast, low-voltage beta waves, while meditative, introspective, intuitive thinking is associated with alpha waves. Again, there's truth to it, but it's a metaphorical truth. The brain is too complex for such simple dichotomies.

In short, we are forced to speak in metaphors, even when we use the terms of science. So why not simply choose our own metaphor? Instead of talking about alpha or right-brain thinking, we'll talk about the "child"—the magical intuitive child we carry within us. In the chapters that follow, we'll be talking about ways to get in touch with this child, and ways to bring back into our practical, grown-up minds the clear wisdom that resides in that hidden part of ourselves.

I'm not claiming that the subconscious is in itself omniscient, but I do believe it is linked to the limitless store of knowledge in what Jung refers to as the collective unconscious of mankind.

Grown-up and child don't need to be in conflict. In the happiest families, they learn from each other. To combine logic with intuition, analysis with creative dreaming, would be to provide ourselves with the full array of tools for success. Matina Horner, president of Radcliffe College, argues strongly for integrating these two forms of mental activity. "A very efficient kind of information processing is probably available to those who have highly developed right hemispheres that somehow interconnect with logic," she says. "Having been trained in chemistry and math, and then moving into psychology, where the questions are more elusive, I've had to deal with this intuitiveness. Even administratively, I've come to respect it, though I don't call it intuition because that word doesn't hold up very well at a board of trustees meeting."

The time is coming when it will. Meanwhile, administrators and business executives would do well to begin training themselves in extrasensory perception. Whether you're an architect in San Francisco or a rug manufacturer in Des Moines, your business planning and your management of employees will be enhanced by access to your full human resources. And what might you do in the stock market (that ulcerous mass of uncertainty) if you had the capacity to foresee upswings and downturns? Suppose you had the ability, combining research with intuition, to forecast where precious metals might be a month or six months from now? As your accuracy improves, you might sense impending takeover bids and move effectively to protect your position. Intuition is one form of "insider information" that is perfectly legal.

As we know, this is not only the age of insecurity, it's an age of insincerity. It's hard to be sure who's telling you the truth and who isn't. What if you could tell? What if you had an inner B.S. Detector that could save you from cultivating business and personal relationships that are going to end up badly?

Successful executives know that proper time-management is the key to success. If only you had access to an accurate sixth sense that would tell you where to pinpoint your energy so that you wouldn't waste time chasing down dead leads. Imagine being able to use your intuition, not to ignore statistics and market studies, but to zero in on the most important elements in them? You could reduce drastically the time taken up by decision-making.

You might also catch new trends on the rise, before the competition has sensed them. You'd know ahead of time in what direction the market is moving. Author Philip Goldberg, in his perceptive book *The Intuitive Edge,* describes the "astonishing speed" with which the truly intuitive mind "can bring together bits of information only remotely related in time and meaning to form the sudden hunch or whispered feeling that we call intuition." It's not magic, it's a faculty we all have, to a greater or lesser extent.

Some of the exercises in this book are a bit like practicing scales, while others are more like acting exercises. But they're all meant to be fun—a lot more like an art class than a tough business course at the Wharton School. In fact, the point of many of the exercises is to take the pressure *off.* A pressured, or stressed person does not have access to his intuition. The book will teach you to think metaphorically—in pictures, imaginative leaps, feelings, hunches. The exercises accomplish this by hooking into the playful side of the psyche, the child within every executive. As you begin to view work as play, you give yourself permission to experiment, "mess around," be spontaneous. And that's when ESP begins to emerge. Intuitive flashes seldom illuminate the paths of frowners and grinds.

The exercises are highly effective, but they require some work and patience. You are learning to awaken a deep and still mysterious faculty, a psychic "muscle" which gets stronger the more you use it. Don't be discouraged if the first messages you get from your subconscious are confusing or garbled. A certain amount of static will remain on the line for some time. But the percentage of accurate messages should quickly increase.

To get the maximum benefit from the chapters that follow, you'll need two inexpensive tools. The first is a small notebook that can slip easily into a pocket or purse. This notebook will be divided into two sections, the first headed "Dreams," the second "Hunches." The uses of the notebook will be explained later on.

The other thing you'll need is a small tape recorder, a machine you can carry with you and get at easily. This is for pretaping some of the exercises in the chapters ahead. It's hard to do a meditation of the sort outlined in Chapter Two, for instance, if you have to read the instructions at the same time. With the recorder, you can close your eyes and listen to your own voice carry you through the exercise.

It's only a matter of time before the corporate world catches on to the practical uses of intuition. Twenty years from now, the principles outlined here may very well have become commonplace in our society. By then, those with the ESP edge will be well positioned for success, while business leaders who have not learned to access their intuitive powers will find it increasingly difficult to compete.

By recognizing this historical shift while it is still in its early stages, and by working to develop your intuitive abilities, you have in effect joined a revolution in information-gathering, corporate planning, office management, and just plain living. It is a revolution destined to alter profoundly the social and corporate landscape of the twenty-first century.

ONE

Getting Started

1 Three Obstacles to Intuition

Within every hard-driving businessperson, man or woman, there is a calm inner executive, the intuitive self, just waiting to be called on. This is the person we would want as our closest adviser.

We may feel this to be true, and yet wonder: If extrasensory perception really is a natural human function, one which can yield fruitful new approaches to business problems, why isn't it more commonly used? The simple answer to this is that intuition is used more frequently than we realize. We tend to think of ESP in dramatic terms: the sudden premonition that keeps us from boarding a plane which later crashes—that sort of thing. But the same faculty of grasping a situation before our senses have time to bring us supporting evidence is used in small ways every day. Indeed, many an executive has called for market research or other studies *after* he's pretty much made up his mind what he's going to do about an ad campaign or an expansion opportunity. The research is used to corroborate the intuition.

The truth is that most creative executives hunger for those intuitive moments and wish they had more of them. For every flash of insight that pushes our business in a new and lucrative direction, there may be dozens of reasonable, well-thought-out strategies that yield indifferent results. What is it that keeps us from more frequent inspirations? Sometimes it seems that there's an inner obstacle, an almost palpable resistance, like reversed magnets, to our reaching the intuitive part of ourselves.

In ancient mythology, the gate to the Underworld or Hades was guarded by a ferocious, three-headed dog. In today's business world, the gateway to the unconscious is guarded by a dog of a somewhat politer breed. But at heart, it too is a three-headed monster. Its three heads are fear, habit, and stress.

Anyone hoping to enter the realm of intuition and bring back its insights must first deal with the beast on the threshold. And the first thing to realize about this creature is that we have stationed him where he is, like a bouncer at the door of a nightclub, and that on some level we have a stake in keeping him there.

Why would we want to block access to our inner self? There are many reasons. We may realize (yes, intuitively), that there's more lurking in the subsconscious than business insights. Emotions are there, for instance, as are all those areas of vulnerability that we have long suppressed. Such worries may be worth a moment's reflection at the outset of this book, because if we are in fact blocking our own way, the exercises and instructions in the chapters that follow will not do much good.

If all this sounds plausible, then we have already come face to face with the first head of the dog: fear. The primary fear is of the unknown, and it's a natural fear to have, even though the unknown is in this case a part of ourselves. Most of us, after all, have been raised to look outside ourselves, not within ourselves. But there's something reassuring in our situation. Our forays into the subconscious are not going to turn up some creature from the Black Lagoon. At best and at worst all we're going to run into is ourselves.

A related fear springs from our ignorance of the nature of intuition. If we follow the exercises in this book, will we go into

26

some kind of trance from which we might not return? Is ESP dangerous? Is it antireligious? Is it like witchcraft?

The short answer to these questions is: no, no, no, and no. Again, the point to remember is that we're exploring ourselves, not trying to contact some mysterious outside spirit. We are not dealing here with a séance, but a science, the science of the future.

There is also the fear of failure and its subtle, reverse side, the fear of success. Whether one or both or neither of these afflicts us depends on our psychology. No doubt there are many causes for such counterproductive fears, but it seems to me that they spring from taking either ourselves or the game of business too seriously. For all the pretentious rhetoric about executive decision-making and the corridors of corporate power, there's got to be a part of us that views the whole enterprise as a game of sandlot baseball. We're in it for the fun of it, because we want to hit the ball over the fence and help our team to win, or we really shouldn't be in it at all. To avoid a challenge in order to avoid failing at it is to give up our turn at bat. Who wants to do that?

Perhaps the most common fear of all for business executives is the fear of looking ridiculous. Will the head of marketing think I'm a kook if she finds out I'm doing ESP training exercises in my office? And if she does, will her opinion hurt my standing or effectiveness in the company?

As Philip Goldberg writes in *The Intuitive Edge,* "People demand *reasons;* they seldom say, 'Give me one good feeling why you think John is wrong.' " To proceed with the exercises in this book and to begin learning how to use our psychic faculties mean becoming acutely aware of how many "reasonable" people there are all around us in the workplace. It's easy to feel intimidated by these reason-bound colleagues. After all, they have reason on their side.

No matter what we tell ourselves, the fear of appearing ridiculous, or irrational, persists. It's a ridiculous, irrational fear, but there it is. For many of us, the only way we'll finally put it behind us is to begin succeeding in our use of ESP. Success never needs to apologize.

That's when our rational colleagues will come to us and say, "How did you do it?"

And we'll say, "I used my intuition."

To which, if they're totally rational people, they'll reply in a miffed tone, "All right, *don't* tell us!"

And here's where the second head of the cunning canine begins to growl. Habit, tradition, the way things have always been done—these are powerful inhibitors of intuition, because, almost by definition, innovation means breaking with tradition. What journalist Peter Edidin calls "the Oops Factor" must be allowed to operate, and most corporations, in their adherence to unquestioned tradition, do not make room for it. "Perhaps the best example of this," writes Edidin in *Omni* (February, 1988), "is one Professor McFadden of Britain's Royal Veterinary College, who back in the nineteenth century told his students that the spores of a fungus similar to common bread mold had once contaminated one of his bacteria cultures, an effect 'decidedly inimical' to the bacteria. If this happens to you, the savant told his pupils, 'the only thing to do now is to throw the culture away.' In 1928 the same thing happened to Alexander Fleming. But he didn't throw the culture away. Eventually the active ingredient of that contaminating mold was isolated. It's called penicillin."

Corporations can either encourage their people to look at data in new ways, or they can subtly pressure them to continue dealing with information as they always have in the past. Continuity and tradition certainly have a place, but the businesses most likely to attract and hold innovative thinkers are those which encourage a degree of rule-breaking, not rigid rule-following. The past belongs to the Professor McFaddens, the future to the Alexander Flemings. Both, remember, were looking at the same objective facts; but one followed accepted procedures and saw only a spoiled experiment, while the other ignored conventional wisdom and perceived an exciting possibility. Which of these people do you want working for you?

As we learn to calm our fears and begin to reevaluate entrenched habits and procedures, we may feel the inner executive beginning to stir. But there is still the third head of the

28

guard dog keeping us from fully accessing our intuitions. This is the ulcer-inducing, snarling-in-the-guts feeling known as stress.

Every executive has his or her own style, and some people feel that stress is not only unavoidable, but is actually desirable on the job. They feel that a certain tension level is needed to get things done. Steve Friedman, the longtime executive producer of NBC's "Today" show, for instance, seemed to operate by keeping his people stirred up, off-balance, and upset. After he left, one NBC employee spoke about the "destructive" atmosphere pervading the show during Friedman's reign, but then concluded that it was probably necessary.

I don't think it is necessary. I think there's a difference between being stressed out and being psyched up and full of positive energy, although these conditions may sometimes look the same from the outside.

There is no psychic, myself included, who can do a reading when he is under stress; and there is no executive who can access his ESP when he's full of tension. Even if one's management style involves the controlled infusion of stress in the workplace, it is necessary to learn how to shut that stress off when one wants to tune in to the voice of intuition. Stress is a form of static. It makes it hard to pick up the secret, intuitive messages we're broadcasting to ourselves all the time.

To some extent, stress may be an inescapable fact of life, particularly in high-powered executive jobs. Say, for instance, you need to make a decision which could have long-range consequences for the company. The deadline is five o'clock today. Stress time.

The first thing you need to do is go into your office or somewhere private and practice a relaxation exercise to get rid of the tension. If you aren't able to do that, or if it doesn't "take," the best thing to do is postpone the decision at least until the next day. You have to know when to be assertive enough to say, "No, I have to take the time to make this decision." Certainly, that's better than making a bad decision. Hiring a wrong person, choosing a wrong communications system, making a half-thought-out presentation are mistakes that can be difficult and expensive to undo.

As a rule, the more important the decision, the more of this book's techniques you should apply to it. They include meditation exercises (Chapter Two), dream imaging (Chapter Nine), creative visualization (Chapter Seven), and use of the pendulum (Chapter Thirteen).

For a start, use the following two exercises for the reduction of stress. They will help you clear your lines of the static we spoke of.

If possible allow ten minutes in the morning and ten minutes in the afternoon for the office exercises presented in this book. But even fifteen minutes once a day should make a positive difference in your energy level and the clarity of your perceptions. Now is the time to take out your portable tape recorder and read the following exercises (specifically, the italicized portions of them) onto a cassette. Then you can play them back, letting your own voice be your instructor. It also saves you from having to figure out how to read while your eyes are closed.

Exercise: Tense and Release

Tell the secretary to hold all calls. Close and lock your office door. Sit in a straight-backed chair. This first exercise is primarily physical and is intended to help you relax.

Now tape the following instructions, reading slowly and calmly. When you're ready, play the tape back and begin.

Loosen your belt, loosen your tie, slip off your shoes. Close your eyes and make two fists. Clench them as hard as you can, to the count of eight. Remember to keep breathing while you do this.

Now unclench your fists, relaxing and opening your hands completely. As you do, breathe out the words, "I let it go."

Next, tense up your whole body—shoulders, neck, arms, chest, buttocks, legs—almost as if you were bracing for an explosion. Hold it, eyes shut, to the count of eight. Don't forget to breathe.

Suddenly, let go of all that tension, breathing out the words, "I let it go." You should begin to feel the energy flowing into you and the stress starting to ebb away. Concentrate on that feeling of energy. Feel the increasing calmness.

The next step is to go through the whole body, one part at a time, starting with your feet.

Tense your feet, clenching the toes tightly, to the count of eight. Relax your feet, and whisper the words, "I let it go."

Tense the calves, almost to the point of cramping, and hold them that way for eight counts.

Then let them relax, and as you breathe out, whisper, "I let it go." Tense your thighs as tightly as you can. Hold it eight counts. Let your thighs relax. Breathe the words, "I let it go."

Clench your buttocks. Pretend they're fists. Hold the tightness to the count of eight.

Then let the tension out of them. Exhale and say, "I let it go."

Tense up your stomach, as though you were expecting to be punched. Be sure to keep breathing (albeit shallowly) while you increase the tension up to the count of eight.

Now let all that tension rush out of you, and breathe the words, "I let it go."

Next, tighten up your chest, breathing shallowly, and hold that tension for eight counts.

Breathe out as you relax your chest and whisper, "I let it go."

Tense up your shoulders and upper arms, and hold and increase that tightness to the count of eight.

Relax the arms and shoulders, breathing out, "I let it go."

Clench your fists tightly. Increase the force, up to the count of eight.

Release the tension in them, shake them lightly, and breathe out, "I let it go."

Now tense up your whole neck and head, grimacing with tightly shut eyes, to the count of eight.

Then let your neck and face muscles relax. Lay your head against your shoulder and let it slowly roll around to the other shoulder and to the back, as you say, "I let it go."

Feel the ripple of calm energy flowing through your whole body.

Now you're in a better state of mind to deal with those problems you were so tensed up about. But you can do still more to free yourself from stress. The second exercise flows

31

from the first and is best done immediately after it. As with the first exercise, tape-record the instructions and then follow them, listening to your own voice.

Exercise: Deep Breathing

Still in your straight-backed chair, telephone calls still on hold, close your eyes and prepare to breathe from your diaphragm, instead of from the upper chest (which is where most of us do our breathing). Imagine that you are not only breathing from your mouth, but from the tips of your fingers and the soles of your feet. You are taking such a deep breath that your body seems to be opening up.

Continue breathing in, to the count of eight. Hold the breath for three slow counts, then slowly (again to the count of eight) breathe out. Keep exhaling until all the air has been expelled. Feel a long moment of total emptiness.

Take a normal breath and exhale.

Now begin the second deep breath from the diaphragm, again counting slowly to eight as you breathe in. Feel the barriers within you fall as your diaphragm fills with air.

Hold that breath for three slow counts, and then gradually exhale, counting silently to eight as you do so. When there is no more air in you, feel the calm emptiness at the center of your being.

Take a normal shallow breath and exhale.

Now begin the third and final deep breath, drawing air up slowly from your diaphragm to the count of eight. Imagine your entire body, every pore in it, is slowly inhaling life.

Hold the breath lightly for three seconds, then slowly exhale to the count of eight.

Breathe normally.

While you are still in this relaxed state, with your eyes still lightly closed, imagine a white movie screen in front of you. It is luminous and empty.

Keep seeing that bright empty screen. Imagine yourself slowly walking toward the screen. It gets wider and brighter as you approach. You feel the sense of whiteness pervading your body.

You enter the whiteness.

A calm white light pervades your entire being. There are no fears, no inhibitions, no mental ruts, no habits of thought, no stress—no obstacles at all to the world of intuition that waits within you.

Enjoy that feeling for a long moment. Feel the emptiness, the condition of no-thought. For these moments, you don't know who your colleagues are, what your mortgage payments are, or even where you are.

Now gradually allow your awareness to shift again to the outer world. When you feel ready, open your eyes.

Welcome back.

2 Befriending the Child

The language of intuition is, to a great extent, the language of imagery. That's one reason we'll be using more and more figurative language as this book progresses, to further familiarize you with imagistic, or holistic thinking. Through intuition, we grasp the *pattern* of seemingly unconnected incidents. A pattern is a complex image. To see it in human events—and specifically in business developments—is to get the big picture, to perceive the overall trend.

There is, as has been said, a part of us that lives in the pattern world, just beneath the surface of our self-conscious, waking mind. It is the part of us for whom past, present, and future are a visible continuum. It's the part that makes connections, unhampered by the conscious mind's self-doubts, anxieties, inhibitions, and narrow paths of thought. It is the ghost within the circuitry, our primal self.

We'll call it the child. It is only a metaphor, of course, just another image, and there are many other metaphors we could use; but the child is very evocative, because there is much that is childlike about this subconscious self. It is uninhibited, spontaneous, emotional. It is what we were before we developed the second self of the intellect, before we learned not to say what we mean or mean what we say, before we forgot what we know.

This is perhaps the reason that Jesus and the ancient mystics taught that the Kingdom of God is within, and why Jesus said in the New Testament, "Come to me as a little child." Come, in other words, in the childlike state, as pure being, before the spiritual signals have been scrambled by the intellect.

Before we had verbal language, we had instinct. Every baby communicates with its mother on a psychic or intuitive level. There is a bonding on what might be called the blood conscious level. This is the sort of connection that our subconscious self still has with the world.

The child is also a friendly image, suggesting the loving adult/child relationship that the conscious mind should have with the subconscious. We are, in fact, both adult and child. We are responsible and we are impulsive, intellectual, and emotional.

Happiness comes from this child within us. It is the child who wants to dance for joy during the peak moments of our lives. We can't, after all, think ourselves into happiness; we *feel* happy. That's why some of our more hardheaded, and less sensitive, business colleagues seem to be leading unhappy lives. We've all met them, the grim ones who are so good at making deals and so bad at keeping friends. We may even have chipped in for flowers when they were laid up in the hospital with bleeding ulcers. Such people are found in every corporation, often clustered in upper middle management. They have given the adult in themselves everything it wants, all the 24-carat accessories of success, yet they've ignored the child. And when the child is ignored long enough, it begins to die.

Yes, we are still talking in images, not in the bottom-line language of logic. But there's a part of us that resonates to that image, because it conveys something fundamentally true about ourselves. Above all, it confirms the essential importance of play in our lives. Children don't merely like to play; they *need* to play, in order to develop into full human beings. And so do we, even in the midst of what we call work. I strongly believe that the most successful executives are those who are able to view their work as a form of play, as a pleasurable and creative endeavor which they can't wait to get to in the morning.

These are the people for whom things just seem to click. They have "all the luck," say their envious competitors. And they do, because the child within them is awake. The child attracts luck because it looks at the world with fresh eyes and invites a friendly response. What we call luck is a complex and largely mysterious phenomenon, involving, among other things, an ability to perceive an opportunity the moment it arises. Such perceptions are given most often to those with open childlike minds, unrutted by routine.

How do we establish contact with this spontaneous, intuitive side of ourselves? There are many ways, and in fact this chapter concludes with an exercise that should help get things started. But first, we need to "child-proof" the office; we need to make it safe for the child to play there.

Here are a few suggestions:

1. PLAY WITH THE OTHER KIDS

It would help, at the start, to avoid sticking labels on what we do, particularly labels like "boring" or "unpleasant" or "scary." Instead, we might try making games out of as many business activities as possible. If we dread a board meeting or an upcoming sales presentation, we might change our mental imagery and look at the approaching event as a tennis match or some other competitive but enjoyable game. It might even be possible to take the competitive element out of it entirely and view the business meeting as a sort of play group.

It does wonders for one's outlook to face a board of directors and see in their faces the children they used to be. Yes, even Chairman of the Board Reginald Gotrocks was, a relatively short while ago, just little Reggie to his pals. It might not be wise to call him that just now, but to *view* him that way can free you up very quickly. And after all, little Reggie is still in there somewhere, behind the facade of the gimlet-eyed boss. Try to find him. If your child can play with his child, you've got it made in the company. You may also find you're having fun.

2. LISTEN TO THE BODY

It may seem just another verbal image to say we have a "gut feeling" that one course of action is right and another wrong for the company. But in fact, the solar plexus (the large network of nerves located behind the stomach), is said to be one of the psychic centers in the body, as well as the seat of emotion and of visceral power. Thus we may have a strong, and accurate, gut-level reaction about a new colleague before we have even seen his résumé. It is through such psychophysical sensations that the child-self within us signals what it knows. It's important, then, that we learn to listen to our body, be aware of changes in our pulse, of involuntary shifts in our breathing patterns, of the body language that others use or that we catch ourselves using in their presence.

The child, after all, loves us and wants only the best for us. It is not a particularly verbal creature, however, and tends to communicate its perceptions through silent little blows of realization, like a fetus kicking inside its mother.

To feel these kicks more strongly, try doing regular relaxation and sensitivity exercises. (The ones at the end of Chapter One will provide a good start.) The body should be kept relaxed but alert. If you're tensed up, or are holding in your stomach like a marine at an inspection drill, you're not going to receive the subtle physical signals from the subconscious.

3. ENCOURAGE THE CHILD

As you get in closer touch with your body, and as you reduce stress and improve meditation techniques, the intuitive self will bring you business insights, as a child might bring you drawings. This is especially true if you consciously include the child as your collaborator, your teammate, in the game of business. Of course, those drawings won't be entirely accurate at first—perhaps more in the nature of stick figures— but be careful not to crush the child's creativity by being too critical.

Praise the intuitive part of yourself when it is even approximately right. When you praise the child, it comes out and smiles and happily offers you another, perhaps more accurate, intuition. When you criticize the child, it runs and hides. How many embryonic geniuses are discouraged by their parents? How many times do we hurt our own child inside by saying, "Oh, no, that's not good enough"?

Of course, you don't want to get stick figures time after time, with no improvement in accuracy or detail. That's when you need to use positive reinforcement, emphasizing what is good about the hunch your subconscious has brought you, and de-emphasizing its inaccuracies. The inner child is nothing if not bright, and it catches on quickly. Practice on little things. When you're in the lobby waiting for one of the four elevators that go up to your floor, ask the child to tell you which elevator is going to open first. Tell it, "Good work!" when it's right, but don't get discouraged or annoyed when it's wrong. Intuition is, after all, a faculty which has lain dormant in most people since early childhood. It was silenced by our vocal and increasingly assertive rational mind, and it must be coaxed out.

One way to do this, as we said, is to invite it to play games. The child can see just about anything as a game if it's presented in a positive light. That's why, when I give real estate seminars, I tell people to imagine that they're playing Monopoly. They're going to put some hotels on Park Place, pick up lots of Get-Out-Of-Jail cards, and collect $200 every time they pass Go. Then the kid inside people gets excited and says, "Oh, boy, I can play this game." And since the inner child is also psychic, it will very often win. A good player to have on your side.

Another way to help your intuitive self come out more is to allow it to be messy. If you're a neat freak this can be a little hard on you at first, but you'll get the hang of it.

For a quick exercise in constructive messiness, close your door, put your phone on hold, clear the desk, and take out a pad and pen—an easy-flowing felt-tip is best. Now allow yourself exactly three minutes to scribble the first thoughts that come to your mind. They don't even have to be sentences. There are no rules except that you mustn't lift your pen from the page or stop writing for three solid minutes. If your mind is blank, write "My mind is blank," or write anything at all, but don't stop to think. When three minutes are up, stop.

Many people find this a physically painful and mentally confusing exercise. Painful because they discover they've been gripping the pen as tightly as they would the safety bar on a roller coaster. Confusing because it's hard to write when you're not allowing your conscious mind time to think. But later, reading the page over, people often find surprising phrases, or expressions of anger about things they didn't know were bothering them. In flecks and fragments, the subconscious has begun to throw some of its intuitions onto the page.

Do this exercise several times a week and you'll discover more and more such luminous fragments. Then do the same exercise, but with a specific business problem in mind—say, the puzzling inefficiencies of the marketing department, or the pros and cons of making a major acquisition. The subconscious will throw out surprising ideas, many of them unworkable. Never mind, keep going.

Another technique that's often useful in encouraging the inner child is keeping a small notebook, one that can slip easily inside your pocket or purse. One section of this notebook will be reserved for recording dreams (we'll talk about that in Chapter Nine). The other might be headed, simply, "Hunches." This is where you write down all the hunches that you've had, from the most insignificant to the most noteworthy and profitable. Later, look through the pages to see which hunches paid off, and why. Doing this not only helps you keep track of the development of your ESP, it also encourages the intuitive child to keep up the good work. The important thing is to emphasize only the positive experiences. To dwell on the failures is to close off the channels to the inner child.

4. BRIBE THE CHILD

As manipulative as it sounds, getting your intuitive side to respond to your business questions can involve a touch of psychic bribery. The free, magical part of us, after all, cares only about joy and freedom. Flow charts are not something it concerns itself about. Although there are ways to turn chores into games, there are also times when you need to reward the child to get him or her to do what you want.

Frequently just loosening up your routine can help. Do little things. When you're in your office on the 28th floor looking down at all the people strolling in the sunshine, your child doesn't want to be cooped up in the office on a day like this. Play hooky for an hour. Go downstairs, buy an ice cream from the street vendor, walk over to the park. Completely change the subject. Feed the pigeons. Go on the merry-go-round. When you get back to the office, sun-dazzled and energized, you'll find yourself bubbling with ideas. Happiness is the amniotic fluid of our inner child; it nourishes the creative urge.

It's a fallacy, in any case, to think that you need to be in the office to be working. You may do your greatest thinking at home sitting in the bathtub. Vary your routine. Take a different route to work. Join a gym and go at lunch hour to play handball or take a swim. Wish less. Act more. Take a chance once in a while.

I don't believe in postponing satisfaction. Delay makes the child in us sad and listless. Do you get one vacation a year? Take little vacations every day of the sort we just mentioned. Do you long to paint pictures? Don't wait till you retire at 65; set up your easel today. Get up an hour earlier than usual, make yourself a good strong cup of coffee, and go into your den while your wife or husband is still asleep. Take out your brushes and paints and start playing with color on canvas.

Are you saving up for a beyond-your-means dream house by the ocean? Fine, but in the meantime, on every nice weekend, drive out to the nearest beach, even if it's Coney Island, and let yourself get a little sun and sand.

Do you have to take a business trip but really don't want to go? I have that problem with trips to New York. The city is just too much for me, and the child part of me says, "I don't wanna!" So I make a deal with myself. I take the child out to a Broadway show while I'm in town, and I eat at some terrific restaurants. It works.

This sort of approach helps put us in touch with ourselves, and that feeling of at-homeness gives the child in us permission to express itself. Of course, as essential as the feeling of well-being is, it's not a synonym for intuition. That requires further work.

It requires, above all, careful listening—probably the most important quality an executive can have. As you listen to others, and to the silent but creative part of yourself, you grow more sensitive. And as your sensitivity develops, you become more perceptive and more intuitive. ESP, in other words, is not a switch you flip, but a growing process you gradually undergo.

First, you'll want to meet this child we've been talking about. Let's try it now.

(As with previous exercises, you will find it useful to read the exercise through, then record the italicized portion on a portable tape recorder. That way you can give the instructions to yourself while you keep your eyes closed.)

Exercise: Making Contact

If you're in your office, have your secretary hold your calls. Lock the door so you're not disturbed, loosen your belt, take off your shoes, sit up in your chair. When you feel ready, turn on the tape recorder and listen to the following instructions:

Lightly close your eyes. Visualize yourself in a movie theater. See the number 10 flashing up on the luminous white screen.

Take a deep relaxed breath, in through your nose, out through your mouth, and go to a deeper, more relaxed state of mind. See the number 9 flashing on the screen.

Deeper, more relaxed. Draw the air in slowly through your nose and exhale through your mouth. See the number 8 flashing on the screen.

Take your time, breathe slowly, deeply, from the diaphragm. Relax, sink further into yourself. See the number 7 flashing on the screen.

41

Still more slowly. In through the nose, out through the mouth. You are going deeper. See the number 6 flashing on the screen.

Calmer. You are moving closer to the spirit. Breathe slowly. See the number 5 flashing on the screen.

Sink to an even deeper, even calmer region. Breathe in slowly. See the number 4 flashing on the screen.

Slowly you breathe in. You feel your deepest self waiting quietly for you. The number 3 is now flashing on the screen.

Everything is slowing down. Everything is calming down. You are quietly open. You are breathing. The number 2 is flashing on the screen.

Perfectly calm. You are ready. You are empty. Breathe deeply. See the number 1 flashing on the screen.

Feel yourself very much in touch with your inner nature. The screen is gone.

You are receptive. You are a receptacle. See yourself as an empty glass vase.

Starting with your feet, imagine yourself filling with a warm, white, soothing, fluid light.

Feel that light move up from your feet into your ankles.

The warm light continues to rise into your calves.

The white soothing light has risen into your knees.

Slowly and warmly it rises into your thighs.

Soon you feel the white warm light filling your genitals.

Slowly it fills your belly.

You feel it rising through your chest cavity, filling all your organs, filling your lungs.

The white light moves out along your shoulders, down your arms, into each finger. Your fingernails glow with it.

It rises up your neck, fills your tongue, your teeth, your nose, your eyes.

The warm light soothes your forehead, your whole glowing skull.

Your body, from toe to head, is filled with warmth and light.

Now, imagine a trapdoor in the top of your head.

It opens up. Blow out of the trapdoor all the negativity, all the fear, all the psychic blocks.

Your head is a chimney, and all the black smoke is dissipating out the top, into the air.

When it has all gone, you are empty of everything.

Imagine the top of your head is still open, and now the same white light as before begins to enter you, this time from the top, moving down. You feel your eyes get warm with the soothing light.

You feel your ears glowing with white light.

Your whole brain is suffused with light.

Your neck grows warm and white.

Your shoulders, your arms, your hands, your fingers are slowly filling with white light.

Your lungs are filled with pure white light. You are breathing the light. Soon your whole chest cavity is glowing with light.

Your belly grows warm with white light.

Your hips, your buttocks, your genitals, are filling with warm light.

Your legs, your thighs, your knees, your calves, your ankles slowly grow warm with pure white light.

Your feet, each toe, each toenail glows with light.

You are complete.

And now, you visualize yourself as a child.

See yourself as a boy or girl about six or seven years old. See yourself as free of prejudices or preconceptions about your psychic ability.

See yourself as a completely free child.

If the child is a boy, imagine he has the qualities of a wizard. If the child is a girl, imagine she has the qualities of a sorceress.

This child has no blocks, no limitations, and can see clearly into the past, the present, the future.

With this child, you can create magic.

Say hello.

Stay in that state for a while, perhaps five or ten minutes, for as long as it's comfortable. Don't rush things. Notice your feelings. Do you feel you have met this child-being before? Does he or she have a name?

Where are you? Is it any place you have been before? Do you smell, sense, see anything? What images come to you? Do you feel more connected to yourself? More relaxed? Let the feelings wash over you awhile.

While in this meditative state you are still conscious, but you are also in touch with your subconscious self. There is a little buzz to it. Call it a light, conscious trance. A dream that you know you are dreaming. A dream that you would just as soon didn't end.

When you have taken your ease in that place of pure being, it is at last time to return to the upper air of waking life. Slowly and calmly, begin counting down from five to one.

Five, four (you feel the chair you're sitting in), three (you become aware of the room you're in), two (you hear the sounds, remember the whole context of your waking life), and one. Open your eyes.

Once you have returned to your daily consciousness, write down the impressions and experiences you've just had. If you had felt yourself to be in a specific place, was it one that had significance for you—a childhood home, a mountain, the ocean? What do you think these impressions are telling you about yourself?

Are your emotions closer to the surface now than they were before you did the exercise? Many people come out of it laughing or crying, which isn't surprising since the inner child lives in the psychic center of emotion. Don't be afraid of whatever may come up. There's no right or wrong in this exercise, no rules. It is all good, it is all yours. It is home.

Get comfortable with this exercise, because later chapters will refer back to it. It takes you to the state in which you'll be doing a lot of psychic work.

3 Your ESP IQ

To gauge your progress in accessing your intuition, it's a good idea to take stock of where you stand now, before applying the techniques presented in the next sections of this book. There will be follow-up quizzes at the end of the book, to give you a general idea of how you've improved.

On the surface, it might seem a difficult task to measure so subtle a thing as your ESP quotient. But the self-administered tests offered in this chapter can give you a rough approximation. In addition to your intuition, you will also be bringing logic, common sense, and life experience to bear on the questions. Such "outside information" may affect the outcome to an extent.

Of course, there are tests you can take, such as those administered at the Institute of Parapsychology in Durham, North Carolina, which attempt to screen out cultural and personal influences. One of the tests used there is the "forced choice procedure," which often involves a "randomized" (i.e., computer-shuffled) deck of playing cards. As John Palmer, a senior research associate at the Institute, explains, the subject's task is to guess the suit of each card, without having any "sensory contact" with it. By chance alone, he ought to get one right out of four, or thirteen correct guesses per 52-card deck. A slightly higher percentage of correct answers could be statistically significant, especially when the test is taken over and over again. Sometimes, as many as 20,000 guesses are made by the person being tested.

Then there are the "free response" tests, among them the Ganzfeld ("whole field" in German) procedure, which involves a sender and a receiver. The sender, in a separate room, stares at a randomly selected picture. The receiver, meanwhile, sits in a kind of sensory deprivation chamber and free-associates about whatever comes into his mind. If he has ESP, says Palmer, "something having to do with the picture will show up in the subject's imagery." Again, many trials are needed to obtain reliable data.

As a busy executive, you may not have the time or inclination for such exhaustive evaluations. Nor is it clear how helpful they are. I asked Palmer if one could do badly on the sort of tests he gives and yet have terrific intuitions in the business world. "Right," he answered. "It's not necessarily true that a person who has a lot of spontaneous experiences will do well on these tests, or vice versa. They're very different environments."

That brings us back pretty much to where we started, to the environment we actually live in. The real world may be messy, but most of us are more intuitive out here than we'd be in a laboratory.

One reason for this is that the child in us is not a terrific test-taker. Faced with the prospect of up to 20,000 questions, this spontaneous part of us is likely to run and hide. Yet this is precisely the part of us that *could* answer those questions. Scientists seem not to take into account the crucial importance of enlisting the subject's inner cooperation. There's really nothing wrong with the tests they administer, but I suspect they'd get more dramatic results if they approached the project as a game rather than as a dry and dreadfully repetitive lab test. It's the game approach that we propose to take here.

First, take a look at the morning paper if you haven't already. Quickly familiarize yourself with the world news section, the sports section, and the financial pages. Don't spend too much time on it. Now put it aside.

Next (this is important), get yourself into a relaxed state by doing the tense-and-release exercise and the breathing exercise at the end of Chapter One.

All right. What follows are four short games, requiring four different forms of intuitive activity. They each take only a few minutes to play. There's the "one-day game," the "next-time game," the "card-guessing game," and the "one-year game." No one game, in itself, will tell you your precise ESP IQ, but if you play all four, the likelihood of an accurate estimate increases. In any case, the results are bound to be suggestive. Have fun.

1. THE ONE-DAY GAME

For this, all you need is a pencil. Try to feel out the answers, rather than simply guess at them.

1. What is the temperature going to be at this time tomorrow? (Call the weather service tomorrow at this hour to confirm). _____

2. What will be the price of gold tomorrow? _____

3. What is the next animal you will see today (whether bird, cockroach, or Bengal tiger)? _____

4. Will the stock market rise or fall by tomorrow, and by how many points? _____

5. What is going to be the headline on the front page of tomorrow's newspaper? _____

6. Who is the next person who will make a comment, good or bad, about your appearance? _____

7. There will no doubt be a game on television tonight (baseball/basketball/football/hockey). Visualize tomorrow's sports page. Which team does it say won the game? _____

8. What was the score? _____

9. Tomorrow morning coming to work, should you carry an umbrella or wear sunglasses? _____

47

10. What color will your secretary be wearing tomorrow? (If your secretary's a woman, what color dress? If a man, what color tie?) _____

11. Who is the next person (not counting your secretary) who will call you on the phone? _____

12. What will be the subject of the call? _____

13. When you step out of the building, what will be the color of the first car you see? _____

14. What is the next piece of music you will hear? _____

15. Where will you hear it? _____

By tomorrow at this time, you will have all the answers to these questions. One of the main values of this game is comparative; i.e., looking at the score you get this time and comparing it with the score you get the next time you take the quiz. It would be extremely useful, therefore, to take a few minutes each day for the next week and run through the fifteen questions above. It's best to do it at the same time and same place each day, so as to establish a ritual. The child in us loves rituals and ceremonies. And by setting one up, you are telling that part of yourself that it's time to show off his intuitive abilities. If you don't want to be bothered doing the quiz over and over again, at least take the quiz one time more when you come to the end of the book.

It's safe to say that if, on this first round, you got fewer than two answers right out of fifteen, you should keep practicing the relaxation and sensitivity exercises we've discussed so far. If you got eight or more right, you can congratulate yourself; you're a budding psychic executive.

2. THE NEXT-TIME GAME

Make a photocopy of this page and carry it with you for the next couple of days, or however long it takes to encounter all the situations that are covered.

1. The next time you go to a business lunch, decide in advance what your client or colleague will be wearing.

48

2. When you and this person meet at the restaurant, see if you can guess what he or she will order for lunch.

3. What about drinks? Is your lunch partner going to order a white wine spritzer, a double scotch, a Perrier with lime, a glass of milk?

4. What do you think will be the first topic of conversation this person will bring up? The terrible weather lately? The Denver Broncos? The business concerns you have in common? Something personal about you? Something about him- or herself? Try to flash on what the person is about to say.

5. The next time you find yourself watching a TV show, predict what commercial will come on first during the next break.

6. The next time you're reading a novel, decide by page twenty how it's going to turn out.

7. The next movie you see, decide within the first ten minutes who's going to get together/get killed/save the world.

8. The next time you go to the washroom at work, predict whether anyone else will be there and who it will be.

9. The next time you're tempted to glance at your watch, resist the impulse. See if you can tell time without it. In fact, leave your watch at home for the next week. You will quickly learn to sense, within a couple of minutes, what time it is.

10. Tonight when you go to bed, don't set your alarm clock. Set your mind instead. Tell yourself what time you want to wake up in the morning and *make* yourself wake up at that time. It really works.

3. THE CARD-GUESSING GAME

This game is a simplified version of the "forced choice procedure" used by the Institute of Parapsychology in North Carolina. Although it can be done alone, it works best with two people. It's more fun that way, too.

Have a friend sit across the desk from you with a well-shuffled deck of cards. Have this person hold up one card at a time, with the back facing you. Very quickly, before you have time to think, say what suit the card is.

Under the table, or somewhere out of your line of sight, your friend is holding a pad and pencil and making a mark every time you answer correctly. Remember, thirteen correct answers out of fifty-two is about what one would expect to get, relying solely on chance. Anything more than that is at least interesting, perhaps significant.

To widen the sample, go through the deck five times, shuffling well each time.

Now you do the same for your friend. The two of you can be a mutual support team.

4. THE ONE-YEAR GAME

For this one, write down your answers on a piece of paper, put it in an envelope, and place the envelope in your safe-deposit box, or some other safe hiding place where it won't get lost. You are, in fact, creating a one-year time capsule, predicting what the world will be like twelve months from now.

1. Imagine that you are looking at the sports pages of the newspaper some months from now. What teams does it say will be playing in next year's Super Bowl?
2. You're looking at a still later issue of the paper. You see the banner headline on the sports section. Which team has won the Super Bowl?
3. What was the score?
4. Now you're checking out *The Wall Street Journal* one year from today. What does it say the price of gold is?
5. Below that you see the price of silver. What is an ounce of silver worth twelve months from now?
6. What is the rate of inflation one year from now?
7. You are looking through the real estate section of *The New York Times* one year from today. What is the home mortgage rate?
8. Flip to the business section of your imaginary copy of the *Times*. What level has the Dow Jones reached (or fallen to) in twelve months?

9. Visualize your television set one year from now. You sit in your favorite chair and tune in to the Academy Awards presentation. Who do you see winning the Academy Award for Best Actor?

10. Visualize yourself seeing the rest of the program. A presenter is opening the envelope for the Best Actress category. Whose name does he read out?

11. You turn on ABC's "World News Tonight" exactly twelve months from today. What is the lead story?

12. Visualize yourself opening *Women's Wear Daily* at this time a year from now. What is the length of skirt that has been declared fashionable?

13. Imagine yourself opening *Car and Driver* magazine next year. What car has the magazine picked as the car of the year?

14. Visualize the cover of *Time* magazine. Who do you see on the cover as next year's Person of the Year?

15. What about yourself? Imagine yourself approaching your own office. What is the title on the door?

TWO

Running a Business on Intuition

4 A Quick Psychic Tune-Up

Accessing intuition is a bit like tuning in to a faint radio frequency; it requires a good antenna, a steady hand on the dial, and some strong, fresh batteries. This chapter is about charging up your psychic batteries.

The truth is, they can get run down. Delving into the subconscious can be as draining as it is exhilarating. And if you don't maintain an adequate energy level, physically and emotionally, you will find it increasingly difficult to exercise your intuitive abilities.

Here are some of the things I do to keep my psychic energies at a high level:

1. EAT MODERATELY

Few psychics can function after downing a heavy meal. On the other hand, it's important to eat something before attempting to meditate; otherwise you may end up meditating about jelly doughnuts. If you've been thinking of going on a crash diet, put it off until after you've worked through the exercises in this book. In general, have breakfast before you leave for work. Eat well during the day, but don't overeat. If you're hungry when you start an ESP exercise, have a cracker or some other light snack.

Most psychics I know avoid eating meat because they feel it's grounding. I do eat meat occasionally, because sometimes I *need* to be grounded. If I've been doing a lot of readings and find myself "out there," a good hamburger may be just what I need to pull me back down to earth.

In general, stoking your body with vitamins is not helpful in your ESP training. The one exception seems to be the B vitamins, which I have found does increase the kind of energy needed for psychic work. However, these supplements should only be taken in consultation with your doctor.

Yogis have suggested that, after having sex, it's beneficial to eat ground nuts and milk. There are, in fact, certain parallels between sexual and psychic activity. Both involve a freedom from the constraints of the body, and both may leave one feeling temporarily drained. After doing psychic work, I find it very helpful to eat nuts and milk. They renew the psychic energy while at the same time bringing one gently back to the outer world.

2. GET ENOUGH SLEEP

Intuition seldom strikes through the fogs of a weary brain. Lack of sleep will quickly catch up with you when you do the relaxation exercises, preparatory to meditation. Instead of having a vision, you may end up having a snooze. Each person's sleep needs are different, so you have to determine for yourself how many hours you need to be at peak energy the next day. If you find yourself preoccupied with business concerns and unable to sleep, go through one of the meditation or relaxation exercises in this book just before you go to bed. It should help alleviate the emotional irritants keeping you awake.

3. MAINTAIN A RELAXED ATTITUDE

I once had a professor who urged his students not to cram or otherwise tense up before an exam. Go out and see a funny movie the night before, he would say. It's good advice, not just for school work, but for psychic work as well. Tension blocks the inner flow. That's why it's probably a good idea to go through the stress-elimination exercises at the end of Chapter One each day before doing your psychic training exercises. Pay particular attention to breathing from the stomach (as very young children do), rather than from the upper chest.

A relaxed attitude is also a precondition for enjoying life. And when you enjoy yourself, the psychic ability comes out more. That's one reason children tend to be more psychic than adults—they know how to play.

4. DON'T MESS UP YOUR BODY CHEMISTRY

Developing the intuitive faculties means clearing the channels between the inner and outer self. That takes a certain amount of commitment, just as undertaking a fitness program demands a commitment. It is simply not possible to do psychic work while under the influence of drugs or alcohol.

Their most obvious effect is to throw your perceptions off. Suppose, for example, you're meditating on oil futures and are getting the number 2, indicating that oil will go up two points. If you've just had a couple of martinis, you may not think the information your inner child brings you is good enough—it doesn't match the rosy optimistic glow you feel inside. "Two points? Heck, let's add a zero to that, make it twenty points."

Smoking is also a drug, though its mental effects are less readily detectable. Do your psychic work first, and *then* go out and walk a mile for a Camel.

As for coffee, there's nothing harmful about a cup with breakfast. But if you're a coffee addict, as many office workers are, you're likely to feel edgy or nervous—just the wrong condition to be in when you're trying to encourage the intuitive side of the mind to manifest itself.

In short, in developing your inner faculties, you want to be under the influence of only one mind-altering agent, and that is ESP.

57

5. PREPARE THE ENVIRONMENT

If you do your ESP training exercises in the office, be sure to arrange not to be disturbed. Close and lock the door and have an assistant hold your calls. Better yet, get to work a half hour early, before the daily madness of office work has begun. Whatever time you choose, do the training at that same time each day. Continuity is a very important element in priming the psychic pump.

Most of the psychics I know use an air cleaner, specifically a negative ion generator, in their offices. It clears the air, almost the way a thunderstorm clears it, and in subtle ways it energizes the atmosphere. Also, of course, if you work in a smoggy city, it's important not to do your breathing exercises in dirty air. You will need, in addition, a good air conditioner bringing in fresh supplies of air. Be sure to change the air filter regularly.

If your office is subject to a lot of noise, you may want to prepare the environment by turning on a "white noise" machine, available at many department stores. Its gentle whirring takes the edge off the raucous clangor of city life. Some machines give out the soughing sounds of the ocean. Or you can buy a soothing tape, perhaps of harp music, to cut down on outside distractions. Eastern bloc athletes are said to favor the largo movements of baroque compositions during their pre-Olympic meditations. Make your own personal compilation tape of music or other sounds that work well for you.

You may also program yourself by taking several deep breaths and saying to yourself as you exhale, "I am shutting out all external sounds." The power of autosuggestion is greater than you might imagine.

6. DON'T OVERDO THE EXERCISING

Light exercise is fine, but you don't want to be worn out or in a sweat when you sit down to meditate. A brisk walk, a short swim at the gym, some sit-ups in the morning are all good exercises because they invigorate without exhausting you.

Many executives nowadays make a point of getting to the health club several times a week for a strenuous workout on Nautilus machines, on stationary bikes and running machines, or in aerobics classes. Or they find a release for their tensions through a vigorous game of squash or tennis. Many people claim that, far from tiring them out, such activities actually psyche them up.

They're right, and I say that what they're going is fine; but the energy they feel is different from the kind of energy needed for accessing your intuition. It's a sort of endorphin high, similar to the sensation of falling in love. Such workouts can be beneficial and the concomitant sensations pleasurable; but in general, if you're into heavy exercise, I would advise taking yourself to the gym later on, after you've done your psychic work for the day.

Also bear in mind the health benefits that flow from the psychic training exercises themselves. Here the evidence is anecdotal rather than scientifically demonstrated, but a great many people I've worked with have said they don't need as many vitamins as they used to think they did; they don't need to exercise so strenuously; they're sleeping better and feeling better. One close friend was suffering from an ulcer before he began his psychic development program. He no longer has the ulcer.

No doubt, the relaxation needed for psychic training is itself therapeutic, particularly for such a tension-related condition as ulcers. But I'm also convinced that psychic energy is healing energy; and when it is strengthened and increased in the body, it heals the body. This is why, as Dr. Bernie Siegel explains in *Love, Medicine, and Miracles,* "terminal" cancer patients are often encouraged, even by medical doctors, to learn the techniques of creative visualization—to visualize the cancer cells, and then to "see" them being defeated by the body's own defense mechanisms.

7. DEVELOP YOUR OWN RITUAL

Habit, routine, and other forms of predictive behavior sometimes seem the bane of a business person's existence. We associate habits (especially bad habits) with ruts and dream wistfully of breaking away from our repetitive lives.

But if repetition can be dulling in some contexts, it can be liberating in others. By programming certain actions, we free ourselves from the need to think about them, and that allows us to think about other things. If we had to relearn basic reading skills every time we picked up a book, we'd have trouble getting beyond the Table of Contents.

The same is true of psychic development. At first, it may be hard to puzzle out the meanings of your hunches and intuitions. But when you get the exercises down to a daily routine, you'll find the inner messages easier to decipher, until second sight begins to become second nature.

In the course of your ESP training, however, you'll find that repetition takes on a second, more profound meaning, related to what is sometimes called ritual magic. The ancient magical chants, whether to mend broken bones or to call up dead ancestors, always relied on heavy rhythmical repetitions to call forth messages from the unseen world. Today, in the air-conditioned quiet of your office, you can replicate something of that ancient magic; but instead of calling up the dead, you'll be invoking the deepest, wisest part of yourself.

Don't be afraid of the word *magic,* by the way, despite the current scientific prejudice against it. The word comes from the ancient root, "magh," meaning "to be able, to have power," and it leads through Greek and Latin to the modern words, "mechanism" and "machine." We're certainly not prejudiced against machines these days, although not many decades ago a machine like the home computer would have seemed very much like magic.

Magic seems to be our word for mechanisms we don't yet understand. Well, ESP is the mechanism of the inner self. It's similar to our personal computer in that it needs to be accessed, or called up onto the screen of the conscious mind.

This can be done through what we might call access codes, which vary somewhat from one person to the next. Nothing could seem more opposite than the terms *access code* and *ritual magic,* but in the present context they mean precisely the same thing. They indicate that you need to *do* something in order to get at the information that is stored within yourself.

As we've already mentioned, one thing you can do is set up a daily ritual, by establishing a regular time and place for your psychic work. This also involves inwardly preparing the mind to be intuitive. Something as simple as washing your hands or sipping a glass of water before each day's meditation will signal your inner self that you're getting ready to begin. As such, hand-washing has symbolic, or ritual, value; but it can also help to break the prevailing energy and open you to a different kind of energy. This is helpful if you've been caught up in office tensions just before your ESP session. Something as simple as running cold water over your hands can help neutralize that tense energy and clear your mental palette.

Next, sit down and, if you've been at all tense, do one of the stress-reduction exercises from Chapter One. Now, go deeper into yourself by doing the "Making Contact" exercise at the end of Chapter Two. By starting each session this way, you are establishing a pattern that will awaken the inner executive and stimulate the intuitive faculties.

8. TRY A QUICK TUNE-UP EXERCISE

If you find you need a psychic pick-me-up during the day, you might try this quick exercise, first developed by Baron Eugene Fursten in the nineteenth century. Stand with your feet spread three feet apart. Close your eyes, rub your hands together, then take a deep breath, stretching your arms out wide to the side. As you do this, feel the energy of the spirit, of God, entering into your solar plexus, and say, "The universal life force is flowing through me. I feel it."

Repeat this three times. I find that within a couple of minutes I feel a sort of "high," a feeling of being charged up. I'm then ready to get into my psychic work.

61

9. SWEEP OUT THE AURA

Even more than magic, the word aura makes many business executives uncomfortable. But whatever vocabulary you choose, it's essential to recognize that the visible physical world has an electromagnetic dimension, sometimes called the pattern body, or astral light.

No matter what our degree of spiritual development, we are all surrounded by an invisible nimbus of electricity. The process known as Krillean photography has shown this force field, or aura, quite plainly. There can be disturbances in this field, like tiny sunstorms, which affect our ability to function fully; i.e., intuitively. At such times, the aura needs a good "airing out," so that the disequilibrium can be resolved. One well-known psychic does this quite literally. She stands outside on a windy day and has the wind sweep over and around her. She finds that this clears the aura.

Salt water has also been found to be efficacious. That's one reason that people find it calming to live by the ocean. If you don't happen to have an ocean in your backyard, throw a handful of sea salt into your bath at night.

There are some psychics who specialize in aura balancing, and if you feel you could benefit from such treatments, you might consult the appendix to this book. The organizations listed there can help put you in touch with a reputable aura balancer.

But there is also a quick exercise you can do by yourself, which some people have found helpful. First, find a place where you won't be disturbed. Then get down in a crouch, almost as though you were about to sprint. Now balance yourself that way, without using your hands. Reach your arms straight out in front of you, then sweep them back as if you were doing the breast stroke. Repeat this movement several times, and as you do, say, "I am the center of light, and only good influences will come to me."

The secret, no doubt, is not in the crouch so much as it is in the mind control you exercise while you do it. You are in effect sealing out, through your own willpower and private magic, any ambient influences that might be harmful to you.

After all, you walk through a sea of spiritual (or if you prefer, electromagnetic) influences all the time, just as your body moves through tides of bacteria, viruses, and submicroscopic organisms. The point of the exercise is to bolster the psychic immune system, so that you don't come down with spiritual sniffles, blue funks, or a case of spotted existential malaise when you'd rather be out playing with the fun-loving child that is part of your central self.

In all these tune-up exercises, the issue of belief need not arise. Most important is a sense of fun and a willingness to let anything happen. For there are mysterious forces moving behind the mundane scenery of daily life; and if you are tuned up, and tuned in, you will feel them stirring within you.

5 Who Do You Think You Are?

A woman I know, a tall, beautiful actress and dancer, became discouraged after years of auditions, rejections, and occasional small, unsatisfactory roles. In her early thirties, she married, gave up performing, and became pregnant with her first child.

Midway through the pregnancy, she had a dream. A winding staircase led down to a cellar where two women were tied to chairs, unable to move or call out. My friend untied them and asked who they were. One said she was an actress. The other was a nurse. Helping the women to their feet, she led them upstairs into the main rooms of the house.

The dream became confused after that, and she woke up. Later that night, she fell asleep again and this time dreamed that she was starring in a Broadway show. The performance was a wild success, the audience rose to its feet, cheering and tossing flowers onto the stage.

Thinking about her dreams, she realized that, as happy as she was in her marriage, there were parts of her personality that she had not been expressing, and that *needed* to be expressed. The performer in her and the healer were kept tied up in her subconscious, unable to find expression.

She also realized that in a sense her first dream made the second dream possible. Only when she'd brought the performer up from the psychic basement was she able to dream of a Broadway success.

The task for most of us is to discover the full dimensions of who we are, and then to allow that identity to surface. Only in that way can we discover what we want out of life. This sounds obvious, but there are lots of people out there who are striving mightily for things they don't really want, while ignoring the things they do.

How do you go about discovering what you want? The simple, perhaps simplistic, answer is to ask. Ask your child self, the dreamer in you, what he or she really wants out of life. Sometimes that part of you will answer in a dream, as it did in the case of my actress friend. Or the answer may come during a meditation exercise, when the noise of the conscious mind is temporarily stilled. Frequently, the first realizations you have concern what you *don't* want. Some deep, inarticulate part of you may simply say "Uh-uh." You may have thought, for instance, that you wanted to stay with your company for your whole career, right up until gold watch day, but something in you suddenly dreads that prospect. Uh-uh. You may have assumed, right through law school and the bar exam, that you wanted to be a corporate lawyer, just like your dad. Then, when it seems absurdly late to change your mind, you realize that that was his dream, not yours, and that you'd never be happy in that line of work.

If you have difficulty discovering what it is you want to achieve, it might be because your belief system stands in the way, and you may have to deal with that first. Many people have negative conditioning to overcome. I'm my own most vivid example. Growing up, I felt that many of my forebears were losers, in one way or another. As a result, it seemed almost a betrayal of them for me to be a success. And for a long time I wasn't; because every time I achieved something, I'd hear the ghostly voice of some family ancestor admonishing me: "Who do you think you are? Do you think you're better than we are?"

Who do you think you are? The question is a basic one,

because you can never hit any higher than you aim, and you can never achieve more than you aspire to. In order to become a success, I had to change my belief patterns, particularly what I believed about myself. Finally I came to realize that I am powerful, that I am a child of God, that I am able to create any world I want.

Many executives, because of negative conditioning early in life, hold themselves back from the upper echelons of success. They were told as children, "Half a loaf is better than none." They were told, "Money is not important." They were told, "Be realistic, don't expect too much."

Then there are the religious admonitions about money being "the root of all evil." This attitude, and its counterpart, the feeling there's something morally admirable about poverty, have a way of hanging on in the popular mind. Really, it's not money but the obsession with money that is harmful. Greed is harmful. Money is simply a facilitator. Even the Lord's Prayer petitions God for "our daily bread." And "bread," in today's vernacular, is money. Yet people who come from a religious background still tend to feel ambivalent about money, especially about the idea of making significant amounts of it. And this ambivalence, on inner planes, inhibits them from clearly formulating their goals and unabashedly pursuing them.

But probably the most common reason so many middle-level executives hold themselves back from becoming upper-level executives is that, somewhere along the line, they got the idea that they didn't really *deserve* great success. You must ask yourself if you fall into this category. Do you think you deserve to be wealthy? Do you deserve to own the company? Do you deserve to hold government office? Do you deserve to have perfect health? Do you deserve to have a long-term loving relationship?

Recently, I was doing psychic counseling for a woman who was starting her own company. The concept looked promising, and it filled a real need in the community, and yet she just couldn't get it off the ground. Upon psychic investigation, I got the strong message that this person had taken a vow of poverty as a monk in a previous life. I know, that may sound a little far out in a discussion of business; but there it was. I explained my intuition to her, and she agreed with me that a vow of poverty was not appropriate for an entrepreneur in the late 1980s. She then formally renounced the vow. Whether her difficulties truly stemmed from a previous life or some other psychological inhibitor is unimportant. Once she had made the gesture of renouncing the vow and thereby given herself permission to succeed, she managed to shake off the hangover from the past. The effect was dramatic. She found the obstacles to her business venture disappearing, and now she's having a tremendous success.

This is admittedly an unusual case; it's far more usual for business difficulties to have more obvious causes. Usually they have to do with a person's world view, or with certain personality problems, such as an inability to get along with co-workers, a failure to adapt to new business conditions, or a fear of taking decisive action. In short, in the business world, almost no one gets done in by others—popular stereotypes to the contrary. People "do in" themselves. And usually they do it more thoroughly than anyone else could have done it for them.

Look around you at what you have and don't have, at where you are in your career and in your personal relationships. The life that you are living is the life that you believe in. You are looking at your belief system.

Look around your office. What do you have hanging on the walls? What are you wearing right now? What do these things tell you about your view of yourself? Are you happy with that view? If you are, you are one of the fortunate ones.

Most people are not satisfied with their position and prospects, or not entirely. But that doesn't matter, finally, because conditions can change. Reality is created by thought, and it can be altered by thought. I espouse the view that what you think about and hold in your heart will sooner or later manifest in reality. Therefore, the business success you have achieved, or the business failure you experienced, or the plateau you have been coasting on are all manifestations of your goals or your lack of goals, your vision or your lack of vision, your intuition or your lack of intuition.

Before you increase your income you must enlarge your imagination. If, at some time in the not-too-distant future, you plan to have your own Lear jet and everything that goes with it, you cannot afford to think like a middle-management person making a middle-management salary, even if that's what you are. This doesn't mean you should become ruthless or haughty—anything but. (In fact, such behavior quickly alienates superiors and colleagues and can lead to your downfall.) But it means that you should be inwardly *ready* for success, and outwardly looking the part. It also means you should be cultivating some pretty well-placed business contacts.

What does it mean to be inwardly ready? It means you've worked things out with your subconscious and have come to a mutually enthusiastic agreement that you really do want to succeed. As we've seen, such an attitude cannot be taken for granted.

But once you are ready, once you've allowed yourself to start thinking big, you'll find that the inner wheels begin to turn. You will be surprised how many profitable ideas come bubbling up spontaneously into your conscious mind. Success often has less to do with persistence than with permission, the permission you give yourself.

Exercise: Projecting Affirmations

One way to speed this process along is to repeat certain affirmations. They can help counteract the negative influences from your past and re-format the great floppy disk of the subconscious. These affirmations can be about anything—whatever signifies success to you. For the sake of convenience, and because it's a common goal, we're focusing on money in the present exercise. You can, of course, adapt this exercise to fit your personal goals. Find a private place where you won't be interrupted, and then, speaking quietly to yourself, make one or more of the following affirmations:

> I am a powerful psychic.
> Money is fun!
> I *deserve* to be wealthy.
> Business is a game.
> I create my own reality.
> I have the competitive edge.
> I choose health.
> The creative force of life is flowing through me.
> I am tremendously talented.
> I solve all business problems positively.
> I reach my goals easily.

Affirmations are not the same as wishful thinking. They are a kind of enabling legislation for the mind; they couple desire with willpower through the incantatory process of repetition. Make up your own affirmations, relating to your own life and business, and repeat them with concentration, but also with a sense of pleasure, several times a day. It's surprising how much they can help keep the spirits up and the ideas flowing. (For a further discussion of affirmations, see the following chapter, "Reformatting the Subconscious.")

Another way to get yourself psyched for success is to find role models in your field. Gloria Steinem's success as a publisher, author, and feminist serves as an inspiration to many women in the publishing industry or related fields. She has shown that even in our male-dominated society women can make every bit as much money as men.

If you happen to be a woman judge and are feeling a bit isolated in the male-dominated world of jurisprudence, you might fasten a photo of Supreme Court Justice Sandra Day O'Connor above your word processor.

Each profession has its own heroes, and your own temperament will determine the ones you find inspiring. One lawyer might pin a picture of Justice William O. Douglas on his wall, to remind himself that idealism is still viable and that even a maverick can reach the top. Another lawyer might put up Marvin Mitchelson, palimony consultant to the stars.

At first glance, this kind of exercise may sound frivolous, but taken together with all the other affirmations and exercises you're doing, it becomes part of an overall experiment in sympathetic magic. By the simple act of keeping a hero's picture in front of you during your work day, you are in a subtle way borrowing his or her power. Magic takes daily practice. It means keeping the goal steadily before you.

Walk into an office as though it is your own proper domain. Take possession of the boardroom from the moment you enter it. As they say in theater, "Take the stage." This is quite different from going in with a haughty or imperious attitude. The theater analogy is apt, because we are, really, talking about scripting the story of your own life and then starring in that dramatization.

Onstage, a bossy, pushy person is not likely to be cast as a hero type. He or she is more likely to be seen as a villain or as a figure of comedy. You want to be the hero of your drama. That means you want to behave admirably, intelligently, with humor and dignity.

Some people, when they walk out on the stage, are mesmerizing; the audience can't take its eyes off them. Others are members of the chorus. We watch the people who project a positive sense of themselves, who dress well but not boringly, who have a sense of flair and an air of confidence, and above all who are absolutely present in the moment. They are *there*.

Look the part. Feel the part. Act the part. Soon enough, you'll get the part.

This kind of rehearsal for success really does help to create the reality you seek. As it says in the Bible, "As a man soweth, so shall he also reap."

It is also a matter of simple logic. If we find a person watchable, attractive, competent, and filled with quiet dignity, we like to have that person around. We want to do business with him.

I first became aware of this approach to business success from a woman metaphysician many years ago. She lived on a large estate in the country. She had a swimming pool, a white Cadillac, stables with horses, the quintessential good life. Yet she told me she'd started out years earlier working in a beauty parlor. One would have been tempted to say to her, back then, "You can't get there from here." But she trained her mind on her goal, acted as if it were already in her grasp, and soon one "lucky break" led to another.

I was initially skeptical, but the more she told me, the more impressed I was. Finally, I decided to try it. I'd always been attracted to gemstones, particularly diamonds, and I began now to focus my attention on them. I cut pictures of diamonds out of magazines, spent time browsing in jewelry stores, learned to use a loupe and to distinguish between a VS stone and a VVS (very *very* slight inclusion). I became a walking gemological encyclopedia.

That year for Christmas I received a box full of diamonds. One could say it was a coincidence. After all, it was from my grandmother's estate and some family member was bound to get the gems. But me? Why not a female relative? I am convinced that, through my concentration on diamonds over the preceding months, I had psychically created the conditions that eventually brought those diamonds to me.

That was my first demonstration that success does come from within you, and that, yes, the powers of the subconscious can lead you to a diamond trove.

Exercise: Who Do You Think You Will Be?

This exercise is a meditation set five years in the future, and its purpose is to provide you with a vision of the successful life you will be leading at that time. In the theatrical or cinematic imagery we've been using, this is your own synopsis of the dream role you are trying out for. It's not a detailed script reading, nor is it a coaching session on how to audition for a role. Those will be covered in later chapters.

When you know who you are, you can begin to learn what it is you want. And when you project a clear image of an attainable goal, you are already well on the way to achieving it. This exercise should help you take the first step.

The meditation begins in the same way as "Making Contact," the exercise which concludes Chapter Two. Again, you'll probably want to read the entire exercise through first, and then tape record the italicized portion, so that you can instruct yourself while your eyes are closed. Also, be sure you are not disturbed during the ten minutes or so that the exercise takes.

Sit up in your chair and lightly close your eyes. Visualize yourself in a movie theater. See the number 10 flashing up on the luminous white screen.

Take a deep relaxed breath and go a step deeper, into a still more relaxed state of mind. See the number 9 flashing on the screen.

Draw in another slow deep breath through your nose and slowly exhale through your mouth. See the number 8 flashing on the screen.

Take your time, breathe slowly and deeply from your belly. As you sink yet further into your subconscious self, you see the number 7 flashing on the screen.

Still more slowly. In through the nose, out through the mouth. You are going deeper. See the number 6 flashing on the white screen.

Calmer. You are closer and closer to the spirit that is your essential self. Breathe in slowly. See the number 5 on the screen.

As you breathe in again, you sink to an even deeper, even calmer region. See the number 4 flashing silently on the screen.

Slowly you breathe in yet again. You feel your deepest self waiting quietly for you. You feel at home in yourself. The number 3 is now flashing on the screen.

Everything is slowing down. Everything is calming down. You are quietly open. You are breathing. The number 2 is flashing on the screen.

Perfectly calm. You are ready. You are empty. Breathe deeply. See the number 1 flashing on the screen.

A silent movie is about to begin. It is set five years in the future. It is about you. You look at the white screen as the film begins.

It is late afternoon but the sun is still warm. You see yourself in a car driving up to a house, or to an apartment building. What color is the car? What kind of car is it?

Are you driving the car yourself, or are you in the back?

Look out the window as you approach the house. Are you on a driveway? What kind of driveway? Is it paved? Is it curved?

There before you stands the house. Your house. Or, if it's in the city, perhaps an apartment building. What color is the facade? How big is it? What style is it? Is it a wooden house? Old or new? Is it stone or brick? Are you pleased with what you see?

What do the grounds look like? Country? City? Trees? Porch? Is there a front lawn? Are there animals?

You step out of the car and approach the building. The front door swings open. Who is there? Do you see any children? Are there other adults?

If there is a person at the door who embraces you, what is your feeling about this person?

You go inside the house. What does the front hall look like? Are there stairs going up, is there an elevator, or is it a one-story building? From where you are standing, what rooms can you see? Describe them.

Take your time and go through the main rooms of the house, even upstairs, if there is an upstairs.

You go into your favorite room. How is it furnished? What pictures do you have on the wall?

You go to the window. What do you see? Trees? The Golden Gate Bridge? Rockefeller Center? A deserted beach with palm trees?

You settle into your favorite chair. What kind of chair is it? What is immediately surrounding you as you sit there? Is there a rug on the floor? What kind?

You are relaxing in your chair, enjoying the life you have built. Stay in this state for several minutes, as long as is comfortable. Then slowly start counting backwards from ten.

Ten. Breathe a deep quiet breath.

Nine. You are saying goodbye for now to this vision, but you know you can return to it at any time.

Eight. You feel yourself in your body.

Seven. Breathe easily, calmly.

Six. Slowly you're returning to the present time.

Five. You are breathing normally.

73

Four. Your eyes are still closed, but you are aware of your surroundings, the desk, the chair.

Three. You feel yourself sitting. You are aware now of your body, and you calmly accept your return to your daily reality.

Two. You have come back now to a relaxed, happy, normal state of mind.

One. Take a breath. Open your eyes.

6 Reformatting the Subconscious

It is not exactly news that we are living in the age of the computer. Executives do their work on them, then drive home to find their children playing computer games in the den. The present chapter offers a computer game of a different sort. The nice thing is, you don't even need a machine to play it on. Call it "Psychic Video."

In some ways, our subconscious mind is strikingly analogous to a personal computer, and vice versa. MIT professor Sherry Turkle, in her provocative book, *The Second Self,* describes the computer as a "metaphysical machine." "You inevitably find yourself interacting with a computer as you would with a mind," she says. One reason for this is that "a computer program is a reflection of its programmer's mind. If you are the one who wrote it," she continues, "then working with it can mean getting to know yourself differently."

My life experience has taught me that we are the creators of our own reality, inner and outer, and that includes the contents of the unconscious. But somewhere along the way, we have lost the key to the file drawers where we keep all that information. We are, you might say, sitting before a computer whose software we ourselves have programmed, but we're having trouble with retrieval.

GERALD JACKSON

For one thing, we can't think of the access code. But even more basic than that, we haven't properly formatted our mental diskettes to receive and display the lost information, even if we knew the code. In other words, we must realign the conscious and subconscious portions of our mind so that they speak the same mental language. If the subconscious understands only images and the conscious converses only in logic, the information buried within us will not be decipherable, even if it could be recalled.

In order to reconfigure our mental diskettes and clear them of dirt, glitches, and obsolete commands, we need to go over them with some simple but powerful affirmations. Such affirmations, if correctly "entered," have a magnetic quality that sweeps away the inner debris and helps to create the necessary compatibility between our inner and outer selves.

Yes, we are speaking in an extended metaphor here. (Remember, we promised in the Introduction that we'd be using more figurative language as the book progressed.) But in this case, the metaphor is so close to reality as to seem almost a straightforward description of the way the mind actually works. Affirmations, if made in the proper spirit, really do help clear the channels and prepare the mind to perform its functions more efficiently.

Affirmations work, declares Thomas Smith, president and CEO of Fairchild Aircraft Corporation, in an interview for *Industry Week* (July 4, 1988). "[They work] on your subconscious, because basically eighty percent of your mental capacity is your subconscious mind. The theory of affirmations is to keep reinforcing your subconscious that you're targeted toward those goals. This basically shows you how to take control of your life."

In this chapter, we'll give examples of affirmations that executives in various business situations might typically use. But it will be more effective if you make up your own affirmations. After all, each floppy disk must be formatted to the idiosyncracies of each individual terminal. The same applies in regard to your own mental software.

Before going further, it should be acknowledged that affirmations don't work for everyone, any more than prayer works for everyone. Their efficacy depends a great deal on one's temperament. A cynical attitude, for example, would be fatal to the undertaking. In order to speak your affirmations with the conviction and force needed to impress them on the sensitive diskette of the subconscious, it's important that you believe what you're saying. It's important, at least, that you're able to engage in a willing suspension of disbelief. In this sense, an affirmation really is a bit like a prayer; without conviction neither one will reach its intended audience.

On the other hand, it won't do to sit before your magical, imaginary computer with your face set in grim determination. The image of the video game continues to be useful here, because the subconscious mind tends to respond when invited to play a game. It's important to strike a balance within yourself, approaching the project in the spirit of play, but without looking on it as a joke.

A final note before we get to the affirmations: it's not enough to speak the words; you must follow them up with action if you want to see results. General affirmations simply lay the groundwork for the real work that is to come: writing down achievable, time-specific goals; undertaking the creative visualization of those goals; and then taking decisive action in the outside world to attain those goals.

Exercise: Psychic Video

First, read through the entire exercise. You'll notice it is in two parts, "General Affirmations" and "Occupational Affirmations." The second part, as you'll see, requires a little preparation before you begin. When that is done, you may want to read both sets of affirmations onto a tape, so that you can instruct yourself without having to glance at the page. I have found it useful to fill up a whole thirty-minute tape, repeating the words again and again. Then, using earphones to cut out distractions, I play the tape at least once a day. People think I'm listening to Billy Joel, but I'm really listening to my own affirmations.

If you're at work, here is one effective approach. Clear everything off the top of your desk and sit down quietly and calmly, with your eyes lightly closed. Start the tape and imagine that before you, glowing invisibly, humming inaudibly, is your own magical computer. You are the only one who can use it; it has been configured specifically to your inner software. This machine is so incredibly sensitive that with it you will be able to read your own mind. It therefore gives a twist to the Socratic injunction: Man Access Thyself.

As you hear the words, watch them in your mind's eye appearing in glowing letters on your monitor.

1. GENERAL AFFIRMATIONS

I am ready to play "Psychic Video."
I am the master programmer of my own subconscious.
My computer can search out and display the answer to any question I ask it.
My computer will access files and subdirectories that I have never accessed before.
If an answer is not in my computer's memory, my machine will come up with the answer anyway, by synthesizing the information it already has.
I have, in other words, programmed my computer to make intuitive leaps.
My computer cannot be entered by anyone but me.
My computer is a safe place for psychic play.
I am open to magic and ready for revelations.

2. OCCUPATIONAL AFFIRMATIONS

This is the place for you to "enter" your own personal affirmations relating to your position in your company and the ambitions you have for the future. Only you know what your situation is. Jot your affirmations down on a pad—perhaps just *five* very strong ones at first—and then read them onto the tape recorder. Phrase them as "I am," rather than "I will" or "I should." Declare your intentions as realities that already exist. After all, they do exist on the mental plane. It just takes a while for them to work their way down to the physical.

The sample affirmations that follow are intended merely as a guide, to get you started.

ADVERTISING EXECUTIVE

I am a genius overflowing with inspiration.
The client is going to rave about this new campaign.
This ad campaign is going to double the sales of the product.
I relax easily, allowing new ideas to flow freely.

REAL ESTATE SALESPERSON

My rapport with my clients is immediate.
I am brilliant at matching personality to property.
I am making promising new contacts every day.
I am enthusiastic and succinct in my sales presentation.
People need me and the real estate expertise I have.

OFFICE MANAGER

I like and respect the people who work here.
I help my colleagues work together harmoniously.
I resolve office conflicts without making anyone feel like a loser.
My efficiency skills are saving the company a great deal of money.
I am creating an environment that my coworkers enjoy working in.
I encourage innovators and office mavericks without letting them disrupt the work of others.

You get the idea. Obviously, drawing on your own experience will allow you to be a great deal more specific in the affirmations you come up with.

After you've practiced these self-suggestion exercises, you are ready to move on to a second form of "reformatting," namely, replacing negative thoughts with positive ones. How many times, riding an elevator to the office on a rainy morning, have you heard somebody say, "Just my luck that I left the house without my umbrella," or some similar self-deprecating remark.

Sure it's an attempt at wry humor and early-morning camaraderie; but what that person is really telling you is: "I am a person who has bad luck." He might find fewer raindrops falling on his head in life if, instead of putting himself down, he constantly affirmed: "I am a person who has good luck, a person to whom good things happen all the time."

"Thank God it's Friday!" Another harmless elevator remark, perhaps, but one which says: "I do not like my job. I can't wait to get out of here."

How different that person's life might be if he or she started the week off, saying: "Thank God it's Monday!"

After all, if you're not doing something you want to be doing, maybe you should think seriously about changing careers. Life is too short not to love your work.

Exercise: Reframing Reality

This is an exercise you'll have to script yourself as you go through the day. For this one, you don't need the tape recorder, only a pad and pencil.

Every time you have a negative thought, no matter how joking the context, turn that thought around and look at it in a positive light. To start, write down five negative statements you frequently find yourself making. Look at them, understand where they come from in yourself, then write down a number of affirmations that rebut your negative assumptions.

If, for instance, in the midst of a struggle for control of sales territory, you find yourself saying, "Oh my God, the

competition is killing me!" visualize yourself hitting the "Cancel" button on your magical computer and wiping that thought out of your memory system. Then enter (i.e., write on the pad):
"I have a competitive edge."

If, in the words of former president John F. Kennedy, you find yourself saying, "Life is not fair," hit that "Cancel" button again. Write down:

"The universe and everything in it is governed by the law of cause and effect."

"Everything that happens to me is the result, on some level, of my own desire."

"I am the hero of my life, not a victim."

"There is no misfortune that cannot be turned into an opportunity."

"There is no such thing as a misfortune."

Negative thoughts, self-doubts, and hesitations cannot survive such overwhelmingly positive responses.

Exercise: Smashing the Negative

As a supplement to the affirmative actions outlined above, I suggest the following exercise: Take a fresh audio cassette, put it in your tape recorder, and say into it all the negative things you can think of about yourself, your personal relationships, your colleagues, your business. Record all your worst fears about everyone. What really gets your goat? Do you sometimes feel inadequate? Like an imposter? Do you feel like punching someone in the nose?

Put it all on that tape, till it is fairly simmering with vitriol.

Play the tape back and listen to all the angry thoughts you have just spoken. Often just hearing these things helps to put them in perspective, exposing your paranoia for what it is. You may even begin to find the tape funny.

Now, go to the tool chest for a hammer. Come back and smash the tape to smithereens!

The reason this often works is that it is a dramatic and physical demonstration of your intention to rid yourself of negative attitudes. The subconscious, which can often ignore a

81

mere thought, is impressed by the stark image of the hammer smashing the tape.

Now that you have booted up your system with positive energy, you are ready to turn your general affirmations into specific goals. This is the next step in the process of converting your aspirations into actualities.

Exercise: Taking Inventory

It's surprising how many people have never taken the time to ask themselves exactly what they want from their career. They just began it at some point and now find themselves somewhere in the middle of it. On the other hand, the effective executive knows what he wants and has designed a program to achieve his goals.

The first step is to make an inventory. What are the contents of your present life? Are you satisfied with them? Do you feel fulfilled?

CAREER

The title of my position in the company is _____.

My goal is to attain the title of _____.
What I actually do here is _____
_____
_____.

What I eventually want to be doing here is _____
_____
_____.

In general, my relationship with business colleagues could be described as _____.
(Warm, distant, competitive, etc.)

My goal is to relate to my colleagues as follows:

_____

_____

_____

_____.

My relationship with the office support staff is

_____.

My goal is to relate to the support staff as follows:

_____.

The support staff's efficiency and general competence could be described as _____.

My goal is to bring up the support staff's efficiency to meet the following criteria: (Be quite specific.)_____

_____

_____.

When my secretary makes a mistake, my reaction is _____

_____.

If I am not satisfied with the way I deal with my secretary's shortcomings, my goal is to deal with them as follows: _____

_____.

When the chairman of the board makes a mistake, my reaction is _____

_____.

If I am not happy with the way I react to the chairman's mistakes, my goal is to deal with them as follows: _____

_____.

What real friends do I have in the company? _____

_____.

Who do I wish was a better friend? _____

_____.

My present salary (including bonuses) is _____.

My goal is to have a salary of _____.

PERSONAL LIFE

I would describe my marriage, or other love relationship, as _____
_____.

My goal, regarding my love relationship, is _____
_____.

If there were one aspect of this relationship that could be improved, it would be _____
_____.

My goal is to improve that aspect of the relationship.
My relationship with my children (if any) could be described as _____
_____.

My goal is to improve the following aspect of my relationship with my children: _____
_____.

My relationship to my siblings, or to my parents, could be described as _____
_____.

My goal is to improve the following aspect of this relationship: _____
_____.

My current weight is _____.
My goal is to weigh _____.
The way I feel about my body is as follows: (Be specific.)
_____.

My goal is to improve the following aspect of my physical condition: _____
_____.

As I look at myself right now, I am dressed as follows: __
_____.

Which aspects of my appearance most please me? _____
_____.

Which aspects of my appearance least please me? _____
_____.

My goal is to deal with the least pleasing aspects of my appearance and make them into the *most* pleasing aspects.

The car I drive at present is a _____.

My goal is to be driving the following car: _____.

My house or apartment could be described as _____.

My goal is to live in the following kind of house or apartment: _____.

Having taken your emotional and professional inventory, you now need to divide up your goals into four different time frames.

ONE-WEEK GOALS

Each Sunday night, before bed, jot down specific achievable goals that you intend to reach by the end of the coming week. Divide these goals into "Career" and "Personal." Hold yourself to your word.

ONE-MONTH GOALS

On the first day of each month, decide what goals you intend to reach by the end of the month, both in your career and in your private life. Write them down and tape them over your desk or on your bathroom mirror where you can see them each day. At month's end, check off the goals you have achieved. Look carefully at the ones you have not achieved and discover why you haven't. Were the goals unrealistic? Or did you not approach them in the most effective manner?

ONE-YEAR GOALS

Otherwise known as New Year's resolutions, these goals set the tone for the twelve months ahead. Again, be realistic, yet demand enough of yourself to make your resolutions a bracing challenge. Be sure to write them down and keep them in a place where you can refer to them. Too often, people forget the resolutions they have made. In such cases, the resolutions do more harm than good, because they make the whole activity of resolution-making seem forgettable and unimportant. Don't allow your promises to yourself to become porous with excuses.

FIVE-YEAR GOALS

These are in a way the most fun, because they allow you room to dream. Decide where you intend to be in five years, what you intend to be doing, with whom you intend to be doing it, and so on. What title will be on your office door? Or will you be in a grass hut in Fiji by then? Be specific, be serious, and keep these goals in a place where you can refer to them (and perhaps update them) easily.

You have now entered a comprehensive program into your secret, magical computer. You are ready to reconfigure your print commands through creative visualization (see the next chapter), and then convert all these goals into realities, "printing" your life out onto the pages of history.

7 Creative Visualization

You're a successful restaurateur. After years of struggle, you're making a name for yourself. There have been newspaper reviews and magazine interviews. But now you need to expand. Just twenty more tables would significantly increase your income base. It takes money, though, to knock out walls, relocate the kitchen, and buy new fixtures. You need a major loan.

You also need creative visualization, not just to plan the renovation, but to help you push the loan through. The way it works is this: First, decide exactly what you want to happen when you go into the bank with your briefcase bulging with financial statements and expansion plans. Define a clear, limited, specific goal. (For instance, having the bank manager say, "Yes!") Then visualize each step to the achievement of that goal.

Get yourself into a relaxed state, then generate a mental image of yourself approaching the bank. How do you visualize yourself being dressed? It's fine to wear corduroys when you're testing out a new recipe for poulet normandie in the kitchen, but not when you enter the echoing marble corridors of finance. Visualize yourself dressed conservatively but with flair. A snappy pair of suspenders wouldn't hurt, so long as they're

87

not alarming to the pinstripers. Is that a red silk handkerchief peeping out of the jacket pocket of your gray suit?

Visualize yourself being relaxed, confident. After all, you've built your business from the ground up, and you have an understanding of its potential. You are the expert. The banker is there to learn what you already know.

Mentally picture the cordial conversation you'll be having with the loan officer. You don't need to pre-hear or pre-imagine every single word spoken during that calm and frank discussion, but notice that at its conclusion you both stand up shaking hands and smiling. Visualize yourself leaving the bank with a check in your hand.

When what you are doing is "remembering forward," you are executing a mental maneuver which leads you back to the future. In the days preceding your meeting at the bank, try to find the time to go through this exercise at least once a day. Pretty soon the near-future event will be as familiar and non-threatening to you as the recent past. It will, in a sense, already have happened.

What you are dealing with here is not wishful thinking, but the construction of a self-fulfilling prophecy. The prophecy will tend to come to pass if the image you wish to make real is highly specific and is projected with sufficient mental force. Researchers are still trying to discover why this should be so. Dr. Bernie S. Siegel in his bestselling *Love, Medicine, and Miracles,* conjectures that "Visualization takes advantage of what might almost be called a 'weakness' of the body: it cannot distinguish between a vivid mental experience and an actual physical experience." The body, in other words, thinks the event has already happened, and it steams right ahead on that assumption, ignoring all obstacles. Dr. Siegel is mainly concerned with visualization as it applies to the overcoming of disease and the bolstering of the immune system. As he writes elsewhere in his book: "Other doctors and my own day-to-day clinical experience have convinced me that the state of the mind changes the state of the body by working through the central nervous system, the endocrine system, and the immune system. Peace of mind sends the body a 'live' message, while depression, fear, and unresolved conflict give it a 'die' message."

It's a fascinating subject for research and speculation, but for our present purposes I'm less concerned about analyzing why visualization works than I am in exploring ways to make it work more effectively.

In my workshops, I always teach visualization techniques. I consider them the most powerful single tool for achieving success in life, particularly when used in conjunction with affirmations and goal-setting. One woman I've worked with has a car dealership in Florida. The market was depressed one year and so was she. The cars just weren't moving. I had her visualize herself at an awards dinner. Her name was called and she stood up to receive a plaque honoring her as the salesperson of the month. A few months later, that is exactly what happened. Now her business is going strong.

It's important to recognize that this is not something new or strange; musicians frequently use creative visualization just before a concert. Many pianists and violinists insist on lying down for half an hour or so and going through their entire concert program in their mind. They see themselves on the stage, playing each note perfectly and with great feeling. No mistakes, no stage fright. They swear this exercise greatly improves their performance.

The same is said to be true of Soviet and Bulgarian athletes before a major sporting event. They meditate, calming their nerves, and methodically visualize every move they will soon be making before the roaring crowd. By practicing the whole program in their minds, they have in a sense preset the dial on the subconscious. They have seen the future just before it happens, and in that way have tamed that future, made it familiar, less frightening.

Scary situations abound in the business world, too. That's why, before you go into an important meeting, it's important to visualize the whole scenario. In your mind's eye, see the face of each person who is scheduled to be present. What expressions do you see? Understand where each one is "coming from," particularly regarding the subject you'll be discussing. Visualize yourself responding calmly and articulately to each question, without diminishing anyone's dignity. Above all, "remember forward" to a positive outcome to the meeting, with everyone smiling and shaking your hand.

Visualization is particularly useful in unpredictable or tension-generating situations. If you need to reprimand a high-level employee, for example, you will want to rehearse the event in private. Visualize this person coming into your office. See yourself calm, confident, and fully informed. See yourself totally free from anger. Hear yourself quietly explaining what the problem is and what the employee needs to do to improve his performance. See the person agreeing with you and leaving the office with his dignity intact.

Note that, although you've primed yourself to anticipate a positive outcome to this meeting, you have not locked yourself into any set of behaviors. Suppose the employee reacts in ways you could not predict, becomes defensive, or angry, or insulting. That's his choice and his way of conducting himself. But because you have been training yourself in relaxation and visualization techniques, you are operating on a different level. You maintain your calmness throughout, remaining in control of yourself and the situation.

What you are doing, in your own way, is a little like the actions of the pilots of Aloha jet Flight 243 back in May, 1988. En route to Hawaii, suddenly the fusilage cracked and part of the plane's roof blew off. But the pilot and copilot brought the plane safely down. Like them, you keep your objectives clearly before you, and you persevere until you achieve a positive end.

A nice thing to realize about all this is that you can't do it wrong. Any creative input at all will result in some beneficial effect. Of course, you'll probably achieve more dramatic effects the more comfortable you become with the process. Just keep in the forefront of your mind the axiom: "I can achieve whatever my mind can conceive."

Be sure, though, that you really can conceive of your goal. You may think, theoretically, that you'd like to increase this year's income from $50,000 to $50 million, but if you have no logical bridges in places that allow you to understand how in the world you're going to make that kind of financial leap, then, really, you have not conceived of it. You have merely wished for it.

That's why I sometimes speak of the turnoff factor. If you ask too much of the subconscious, you overburden the fun-loving magical child-self, and it wants to run and hide. If you intend to be a body builder, start with ten- or twenty-pound weights. Don't pile on two hundred pounds and rip your muscles. Set goals that are realistically optimistic.

An interesting aspect of creative visualization is the way in which it brings the two hemispheres of our brain into close cooperation. The left, or logical, is in a sense programming the right, or imagistic, side. You wouldn't want your spontaneous, image-generating side to run away with you like a kid in a candy store. The child needs the guidance of the adult, par-ticularly when they're both contained within the same person.

If, for example, you are one of those who shares the great American romance with the automobile, your child-self may want to own this Peugeot, that Rolls-Royce, and a classic '65 Chevy besides. If you managed to acquire them all, you'd have a used-car lot. Your conscious, left-brain thinking decides what car is actually suitable to your present lifestyle—then it bar-gains a bit with the right side, which demands personalized plates and a car phone.

In practicing creative visualization in your own life, keep in mind the following seven points:

First, attitude is a powerful magnet. You attract those qualities that correspond to what is going on inside you. If you have an underlying anger, you will constantly find yourself in battles. If you see things going wonderfully well for you, they will tend to go well. Keeping a generous, positive attitude is not just a nice, sociable thing to do; it is a way to preprogram yourself for success.

Second, accept reality. Don't try to "visualize away" what already exists. The idea is not to resist the present moment but to shape what is yet to come. This means learning acceptance while maintaining optimism. All right, so the sales presentation did not go well this morning. Examine dispassionately what happened and what didn't happen, and then let it go. Next week's presentation will be a smash!

Third, learn to accept the reality of your own emotions, allowing yourself to experience freely whatever feelings are going through you. If you can't stand your boss, there's no point in "visualizing" that you love the guy. It's more constructive to analyze the source of the conflict. Once that is understood, it should be possible to script an entirely realistic scenario in which that conflict is resolved. It is at that point that creative visualization can help.

Fourth, construct your visualizations carefully and clearly. Keep them short, simple, specific. Know the precise outcome you are working toward. Photography provides a useful metaphor here. You need to focus exactly and leave extraneous objects out of the frame, or you'll end up with a blurred or badly composed print.

Fifth, throw the full force of your imagination into your visualizations. A lot of people have the dream but not the drive. The image of success you see before you needs to be magnetized by your will, desire, confidence, and personal forcefulness. There are few forces in the world equal to that of human determination.

Sixth, be absolutely sure that you really want the object or event that you are visualizing, because you are likely to get it. Dream big, but also, in a sense, carefully. It is one of the commonplaces of corporate life that people strive for goals which, when attained, turn to ashes in the mouth. (You might refer to Chapter Six, where we discuss setting goals.)

Finally, recognize that creative visualization is a help but not a guarantee. Not every image you magnetize with desire and determination is going to manifest itself. For instance, say that you want a large raise this year, instead of the five percent the company usually gives. You don't visualize a hundred-percent raise, because you want to be realistically optimistic in your projections. You decide on twenty percent. You do the whole thing right, even to visualizing the boss smiling and saying yes. But when the time comes, the boss doesn't say yes; he says five percent, as usual.

Did you fail? Not necessarily. If you direct a strong visualization at a company and it does not respond, the problem could be with the company, not with you. Maybe it means that you should think of moving to another division, or to a different organization altogether. Your "failure" may be the best thing that could have happened to you, if it gives you the push you need to move your career forward.

Creative visualization can be a powerful tool in your personal life, too. It can be very effective, for instance, in keeping you on track with a weight-loss or exercise program. Visualize yourself as a person of invincible willpower. View the exercise regimen as a game, not as a penance. See yourself clearly the way you intend to look after one month on your diet. Sculpt that image in your mind and hold it there with confidence and pleasure. (A grim attitude, or other negative feelings, can work counter to the effect you desire.)

It can also be a help with phobias. If you have an unreasonable fear of elevators or of airplanes, you can "desensitize" yourself to these feared objects by visualizing wonderful experiences with them. (On travel fears, see Chapter Eighteen.)

Creative visualization can have an equally dramatic effect on your love life. Many executives, men as well as women, have invested so much of their life energy (not to mention time) in their careers that they've allowed their love lives to languish. It is a staple of talk shows that women executives in their thirties are suddenly hearing biological clocks ticking away inside them, as if they were walking time bombs. They want commitment, love, marriage, children, and they want them last week.

If this scenario sounds familiar, the first thing you need to do is get rid of the desperation which underlies such thinking. Desperation (and its milder form, anxiety) is a fear of negative results; and what you fear you attract.

Do a relaxation exercise. Find your way to your calm central self, the part of you that is beyond anxiety, and *know* that that is you. On that level, you are the creator, not the victim, of the events in your life; and that includes your relationships with others. That part of you is never hurried, never late. You are on God time.

While in the meditative state, consider your love relationships. If you're in a relationship that is unsatisfactory, you need to ask yourself why. What do you get out of it? You must get something, because on a deep level we only do what we want to do. (Martyrdom, for instance, is a very powerful reward for some people.)

If you're in no relationship right now, ask yourself why you have chosen to keep other people at a distance, and whether you are now *really* ready to let them in.

Meditate honestly on what qualities you tend to bring out in others, and what qualities you want a partner to have. As Shakti Gawain expresses it in *Creative Visualization,* "If you truly *desire* to have deeply fulfilling, happy relationships in your life, if you *believe* that it is possible for you to have them, and if you are willing to *accept* that happiness and satisfaction, then you can and will create relationships that work for you."

For some reason, it is that last hypothetical that gives people the most trouble. Learning to accept happiness is hard if you don't think you deserve to be happy, or if you're afraid that opening yourself to happiness means making yourself vulnerable to betrayal. All these inner twists and turns have to be gently unwound, straightened out, and examined. Only then, when this internal accounting is completed, are you ready to apply creative visualization, because only then do you know what you want.

Now, visualize that desired relationship—not some fantasy "dreamboat," but a person with the qualities that answer to your deepest affinities. See yourself as a person with the courage to trust, a person who does not need to sabotage himself or herself anymore. A person who is lovable.

Exercise: Projecting a Visualization

This is an exercise you will have to script for yourself, since it is your own life that it concerns. Also, the imagery you choose should be your own. "It must be an image that that person can see in the mind's eye as clearly as something seen by the physical eyes," writes Dr. Siegel in *Love, Medicine, and Miracles.* "It must be an image with which the [person] feels completely comfortable."

Pick a problem area in your daily business dealings and write out a specific scenario for dealing with it. Then concentrate on the images in that scenario, projecting them with force and precision onto your mental screen.

Here's a sample situation, which you might use as a model:

You are very close to concluding an important deal. Before you enter the final negotiating meeting, see clearly in your mind the provisions that you want incorporated in the document you will all sign.

Visualize yourself arriving at the meeting. Your appearance and your self-confidence speak for you before you even say hello. If you have access to the room where that meeting will take place, go and visit it beforehand, when no one's there. Fill it with your positive thoughts.

Find out who will be attending the meeting. Clearly visualize each person there. Go through the whole negotiation in your head, including the anticipated reactions from the others.

See yourself answering all questions confidently and with a feeling that you are helping and teaching others, free from any trace of defensiveness. See this upcoming meeting as an experience to savor and enjoy.

Now, visualize yourself taking your pen from your jacket pocket and signing the deal. Everyone else signs it, too, and there is a sense that everyone has come out a winner. You shake their hands.

Congratulations all around.

8 ⋮ Seeing What Isn't There

$\mathbf{T}$rustworthiness, motivation, sociability, competence, these are all valued qualities in an executive. But the quality most highly prized of all—prized and feared—is originality, the ability to generate new ideas, perceive new trends, design new services and products. There are a hundred dependable middle-level executives for every one who can come up with a fresh idea. Such a person is quickly perceived to be indispensable to the company.

No book can make you into an original thinker; but it is possible to suggest ways to clear away the obstacles you may have placed in your own mental path. One such obstacle is over-reliance on the rational mind. Remember the Edsel. The Ford Motor Company has never lived down that design disaster back in the '50s. It remains the symbol of logical thinking unaided by inspiration. What research was done, what studies made! As a gesture toward the intuitive side of the brain, the company actually hired a poet, Marianne Moore, to come up with a name for the car. But in the end the company ignored her suggestions, which included "Silver Sword," "Arc-En-Ciel," and, wonderfully, "Utopian Turtletop."

If you learn to develop and rely on your intuition, you may at times come up with something fanciful and turtletoppy, but at least it will have the iridescence of originality about it. It won't be an Edsel.

The idea, of course, is to combine both intuition and logic, to generate the most exotic dream car ever imagined, and then go back over the design to be sure the seat belts work and there's a place for the spare tire.

What makes originality so difficult to analyze is that it covers its tracks very quickly, converting the unheard-of into the commonplace. Every schoolboy knows that the world is round, but that fact wasn't obvious before Columbus defined conventional wisdom and set sail for the East by heading West.

Edison is another grand exemplar of the innovative mind. What could be simpler than to look at a gas lamp and say, "Why can't we do this with electricity?" What could be more obvious than to look at those flip-the-picture books and say, "Why can't we make pictures move on a screen?"

Then, of course, after motion pictures became commonplace, someone came along and said, "Why can't we put sound with the pictures?" And later—again obviously—another someone said, "Why do these pictures have to be in black and white? What about color?"

You know you have an original idea when half the people say, "You're crazy!" and the other half smack their foreheads and say, "Why didn't I think of that?"

Intuition does not, however, strike miraculously like lightning on a sunny afternoon. Almost always, the clouds have been brewing for quite a while. The inventor has been in an inventing frame of mind for months or even years, coming up with duds, absurdities, and marginally useful ideas. The same is true of creativity in the context of business. To come up with a striking new marketing concept, you need to have developed the creativity habit over a period of time. To see how this works, consider four different kinds of executive tasks requiring the generation of original ideas:

GERALD JACKSON

1. CREATING AN ADVERTISING CAMPAIGN

If you're in advertising, you already know the importance of priming the creative pump with daily attempts to come up with new concepts and designs. You also know that it doesn't always work. There are days when the paper in the typewriter, or on the drawing board, seems like a blank, reproving wall, impossible to surmount. Everything you come up with seems derivative and dull. You are more aware than ever at such times of how tight your deadline is.

The first thing to do is to dissociate yourself emotionally from the problem. Don't give it strength by thinking, "Oh my God, I've got a writing block!" By declaring the existence of a block, you have just constructed one and dumped it in your driveway. So avoid such labels.

Tell yourself what you already know: that you are a creative spirit who is capable of brilliant work, and that you will, in fact, succeed in the present project. In other words, use affirmations such as those discussed in Chapter Six. They will help get you in the right mind-set. I would avoid scare words such as "deadline," even in a positive statement such as "I easily meet my deadlines." Why not change the phrase around and say: "I easily meet my lifelines"?

You have already seen and digested the basic market research on the product or service for which you are creating this campaign. You also understand the needs and (especially) personality of the corporation which has hired you. In addition you will, by now, have done some brainstorming with the other "creatives" working on the account. Still nothing terrific in the way of ideas. You find yourself making lots of trips to the coffee urn, the mailroom, the water cooler, the bathroom, anything to avoid the void.

One good approach to the problem is to go through the exercise, "Making Contact," which concludes Chapter Two. That's the one in which you visualize a screen before you and slowly count down from ten, relaxing more and more as you go. Finally, you get to the point where you visualize yourself as a

98

child, as a boy or girl of about six years. If a boy, you are a wizard, if a girl, a sorceress.

Speak to this child quietly. Ask him or her to play a game with you, an advertising game. Keep your mind open, don't reject anything. Just write the images and ideas down on a piece of paper as fast as they come to you. Keep saying to the child part of you, "That's great! Anything else?"

When you feel you've gone as far as you can with this session, be sure to thank the child. Then start counting slowly backwards from ten to one, ending with a return to your physical surroundings.

Only then will you take a look at what you've scribbled. Are some of the images useful? Do they suggest other imagery that might be appropriate? The editing function of the mind can now shape this raw material; or it might end up rejecting all of it. At the very least, you have loosened the creative logjam and started the images flowing. A second visit to the child, a few hours later, might yield more usable stuff. Even wizards and sorceresses need a little practice to get the hang of an advertising campaign.

Another way to get things moving is to give yourself permission to be messy, to make mistakes, to write down utter nonsense. Many creative people block their own inspiration by expecting it to appear in a presentable form. A way to get past this is to do the scribble exercise described in Chapter Two. Get a pad and an easy-flowing pen. Decide on a general subject—probably the product or service you are creating the ads for—and scribble incessantly for exactly three minutes. No matter what, do not lift your pen from the page. Never mind spelling or sentence structure. Least of all, don't worry about making sense. You might even, for the fun of it, try to avoid making sense. Afterwards, look over what you've done. Do any striking images gleam up at you from the page?

Yet another approach begins with a relaxation exercise. (One of those at the end of Chapter One will do.) When you have reached a state of deep relaxation, imagine yourself walking down a path in the woods. You come to a clearing in which stands a workshed. No one will disturb you there. It is your secret place. You enter and look around, visualizing the details of the furnishings and layout. Now, see yourself settled comfortably in, ready to work. Suggest the name of the product you want to find a campaign for. What words or images suggest themselves?

By building yourself this imaginary sanctuary, you are in a sense creating a separate subdirectory in the mind's computer, a protected sector where no computer hacker can intrude. Any list you enter will remain there in a file, waiting for you (you alone) to retrieve it. Here, then, is yet another image-cluster to invoke. Like the image of the sylvan workshed, the computer metaphor suggests that creativity is not an event so much as it is a place, a part of the mind one goes to for Garbo-like seclusion.

2. DEVELOPING A NEW LINE OF PRODUCTS

Few corporate decisions are more crucial than the determination of what new products and services to develop. The Coca-Cola Company decided that a hundred years of fantastic success was not enough, and that the old formula could be improved. The result was New Coke. It tested out pretty well, but tradition is not a test. No one used plain old horse sense, much less ESP, to find out if people across America wanted to change something they had grown up with and liked just fine. They didn't.

Meanwhile, at the giant company Coleco the opposite situation occurred. Coleco's line of home computers had been generating huge profits, but a series of managerial mistakes weakened their market position and profits began to tumble. The company was said to be in real danger of collapse. Then Coleco came up with a new product—a doll, of all things—and profits once more zoomed. For years afterwards, just about every little girl in the country was begging her parents to buy her a Cabbage Patch doll, complete with birth certificate, fancy wardrobe, and hefty price tag.

Two companies, that were at opposite experiences. The moral of one: If it's not broken, don't fix it. Of the other: If you're facing certain death, don't be afraid to try something new.

If you're a CEO or board member of a profitable company looking to diversify, you'll want to bring all the information you have to bear on the question of new products and services. But in addition to market profiles and expert advice, the open-minded executive will consult his own intuition. The meditation exercise, "Making Contact," in Chapter Two, remains a powerful tool for accessing your inherent wisdom. Just ask the wizard or sorceress within you to have a go at the problem. Or go to that imaginary retreat in the woods and commune with your inner self about it.

The point of such exercises is to prompt the subconscious to react; so whatever method works for you, no matter how odd it might seem to others, use it. Some people, for instance, find it useful after reaching the meditative state to visualize a fishbowl filled with slips of paper. Keeping in mind the question you want answered, imagine yourself slowly reaching into the bowl and pulling out a paper. You unfold it and read what it says. The new product you see written there may be your company's equivalent of the Cabbage Patch doll.

Another way of getting a reaction from the subconscious is to imagine a flashbulb going off and Polaroid camera whirring. The print emerges, but at first you can't make out the picture. Gradually, the print darkens and an image appears. What is it? Can you make out the new product line your company will be launching?

3. RELOCATING YOURSELF OR THE COMPANY

Another crucial corporate decision has to do with finding the best location to do business. New York City used to be a mecca for large corporations, but taxes, real estate prices, and environmental considerations have driven many companies into the suburbs or even into the countryside. Now industrial parks bloom beside Kansas cornfields and the ivied walls of Princeton. There are all kinds of practical considerations to take into account, and for them you will need (as always) to use a certain amount of practical left-brained thinking.

But your intuition will tell you if you'll be *happy* with the move, if your company will prosper there, if the deal feels right. Remember, the *Titanic* was an exciting, high-tech "unsinkable" ocean liner, and everyone wanted to be aboard for its maiden voyage. Well, almost everyone. There were a few intuitive people who decided at the last minute to stay home.

If you are one of those involved in making the decision about relocating your company, you will find that talking it over with your inner self while in the meditative state can help you spot flaws in the plan that you might not otherwise have seen. Withdrawn from outside influence, you may realize how much pressure is being brought to bear on the decision-making process, and by whom. The most compelling recent example of such pressure is the Challenger explosion. This tragic event, which almost put an end to the shuttle program, might not have occurred if certain key people had not caved in to political and financial pressures. Safety, it turned out, was not the only consideration, but was weighed against such matters as the amount of money it cost every time a launch was delayed. If those making the calculations had meditated on the possible consequences, I am certain the shuttle would not have been launched that day.

Now, suppose that it is just you, not the whole company, that is considering moving. It is still essential to ask your intuitive side about the intangibles. How will you *feel* living in that new place? Do you think your children will be happy there? What is your feeling about the schools? And what about your spouse, and his or her career? Is anyone you love going to be affected negatively by this career move? If so, it may not be worth it. These are matters that can be dealt with fully and truthfully in the precincts of your own soul, away from the excitement of the outer event.

4. RESTRUCTURING THE COMPANY

Gorbachev's program of *perestroika* is probably one of the largest restructuring jobs ever attempted—making a whole society learn to operate in a different and more efficient manner. But even a small or midsize company can benefit from a dispassionate examination of its methods and goals. With many companies, including such giants as the Chrysler Corporation or CBS, restructuring is a brutal necessity.

If it is your job to supervise the restructuring of your company, you know that some employees are likely to be hurt by your decisions. You've accepted that going in.

Your team of experts has gathered all the financial data, made its efficiency report, and has determined that there are a number of weak spots in the company's operations. It begins to look as if a whole division of the company is inefficient and increasingly inessential and should probably be sold off.

Fine, whatever you discover about the company needs to be known and analyzed, and may need to be acted upon. You see yourself, properly, as a surgeon who is examining a patient's X rays.

But before the surgeon makes an incision, it is essential that he or she understand the nature of the person being operated upon. Many doctors still make the mistake of thinking they are treating a disease, rather than a person who happens to have a disease. Holistic thinking is needed, whether the subject is the physical body or fiscal policy. The guy in the white mask and the guy in the green eyeshade must not allow themselves to hide their faces from the human reality of what they are doing.

This is not a matter of generosity so much as it is a matter of long-range self-interest. After Laurence Tisch took over as head of CBS, for instance, the fellows with the green eyeshades looked around the News Division and found decades of wasteful and extravagant practices. Clearly, some streamlining was in order; but the efficiency experts did not seem sensitive to the venerable news traditions of CBS. When Tisch's people began their wholesale firings and the closing of foreign bureaus, the bottom line started to look better, but at the cost of a tremendous drop in morale. The same problem began appearing in other divisions of the company.

Before undertaking to restructure your company, I recommend going into a meditative state, contacting your calm inner self, and asking him or her what your company really stands for. Then ask what you can do to safeguard that quality, while still making the changes that must be made.

Your task, as we mentioned, may oblige you to inflict some pain, and you must do so dispassionately, with a steady hand. Emotional involvement, then, would seem to be something to avoid. Indeed, it is for that very reason that surgeons generally do not operate on family members. While still in the quiet zone of meditation, ask your inner self if you are being truly dispassionate or if you are putting your own spin on the data because of some private stake you may have in the results.

Keep in mind as well that detachment is not the same as indifference. If you find that a division of the company is semiredundant, do a meditation on how it can be restructured with the least possible disruption of employment. Many companies, during troubled economic times, have been forced to close plants. But while some leave town, causing sudden widespread unemployment, others retrain and seek to find employment for the workers they must let go. Is this altruism?

Was it altruism or brilliant business thinking when Northwestern Mutual Life gave a bonus to existing policyholders by increasing their insurance coverage and raising future cash values without hiking premiums? Insurance expert Joseph Belth, quoted in *Forbes* magazine (February 22, 1988), declared, "It is rare indeed to find a company devoting such effort to a program whose primary purpose is to improve the position of existing policyholders rather than to attract new policyholders." But the payoff has been the widespread perception that Northwestern is genuinely concerned for its customers. The payoff is that new customers are attracted by the reputation the company has been building.

Sometimes the way to cut costs is to spend a little money—because it is seed money. Looking beyond the obvious, you are able to see that building a business means building a reputation. It means standing for something. That may be worth some investment.

So if you are restructuring your company, restructure your thinking first. Tap into the genius of your own inner executive. You may end up transforming not only the company, but the lives of everyone in it, including your own.

9 Dream Imaging

Dreaming is probably the most accessible and most underused psychic resource we have. Every morning we wake up with fragments of intuitive vision within our grasp; yet too often we neglect to fit those fragments together into a coherent picture. It is a resource that everyone can use, even those who are convinced that they don't dream. Studies of rapid eye movements (REMs) and other activity during sleep strongly suggest that all of us dream. And with practice we can learn to bring more and more dreams across the threshold into waking consciousness.

Perhaps one reason we're not more successful in this task is that, on some level, we don't want to be. It's possible we're afraid of what might come through. Deep-sea divers, after all, may come up with dripping trophies, or they may be eaten by sea monsters. To the waking mind, the world of dream is the Deep; we want the trophies (the price of gold being what it is), but can do without the monsters, even if they're our own self-created monsters of fear.

And so we employ a censor. Any dream, before we allow ourselves to remember it, must pass under the scrutiny of an internal border guard, whose job is to keep dangerous psychic contraband from entering the conscious mind. Morally unacceptable impulses or unendurable primal fears are frequently stopped and searched and sent directly back to the subconscious.

Some of our dreams, then, get suppressed before we have a chance to remember them. To gain access, we need to issue new instructions to the monitor patrolling our inner borders. After all, we are the chief executive of our lives, and we can revamp our own infrastructure to suit our needs. But we have to be convinced that we will not be harmed by relaxing our censorship, that the contents of the unconscious are our valuable personal property and can only help us. The truth is, there is simply no benefit in keeping submerged truths from the light of conscious thought. Isn't that, after all, what suppression is: an unwillingness to know what we know?

To those readers who are leery of the subconscious and all its nonlogical and confusing contents, a few brief affirmations before bed might prove helpful:

I accept whatever is within me.
I love myself just as I am.
The subconscious is my place of safety, my secret home.
Sleep is an adventure from which I will return rich in wisdom.
I allow myself to dream about anything.
I allow myself to remember any dream, without restriction.
My dreams help me to grow.
I am a magical child.

If some dreams are willfully suppressed, most others are carelessly forgotten, because we don't value them, or because we wake up to the jarring sound of an alarm clock, or because our daytime concerns and worries immediately crowd into our mind. We also tend to forget confused or jumbled dreams, those without a clear message or imagery. Since most of us haven't yet disciplined our dreaming faculty, it's not surprising that so many of our dreams seem confused.

And yet, what a resource dreams are, when properly developed and encouraged. I frequently resort to dream in order to find out things my conscious mind doesn't know. In a recent move to a new house, for instance, I misplaced some important papers, including my will and insurance policies. Three months later I still couldn't find them. Going to bed one night, I asked the subconscious to favor me with a dream that would give me some indication where to look. The dream I got could not have been more literal. I saw myself walking to my car, opening the glove compartment, and finding the papers. When I woke up, I ran out to look. Sure enough, there they were. Then I remembered that I'd stuck them there for fear they'd be misplaced if I had packed them in a box. The memory of that action was still in my subconscious, although my conscious mind had forgotten it.

It's easy to understand how dreams can help you access this kind of once-conscious information. The fascinating thing is that dreams can also help you with information you *never* knew consciously. To which of the three lowest bidders should you award the building contract? You've done all the research, interviewed them all, but the logical part of your mind can't perceive the advantage of using one rather than another. So you decide to sleep on it. You get into a calm state before bedtime, either through prayer or a relaxation exercise; you then ask yourself the specific question, Which of these three final bidders is best for our company? Ask it three times, to impress the subconscious with the importance of the request. Then go to sleep.

The answer may come that night or the next night (like Peter Pan, the subconscious is sometimes lax about keeping appointments); but it will come at some time, in some form. Perhaps the indication will be indirect. You may dream that you're in a wine shop picking out a bottle of Lillet, and you see one of the three contractors carrying an aquarium through the store. On awakening, you scratch your head and say, "What does that have to do with anything?" Then you may think further: "wine," "alcohol," "aquarium": *Drinks like a fish!* Further investigation reveals that the contractor you saw in the dream has a severe alcohol problem. You had no conscious way of knowing that, but because of the sensitivity of the psychic antennae, you had a *subconscious* way of knowing.

The language of dream is usually visual and dramatic, rather than verbal and logical, so that if you ask the subconscious whether or not your corporation will be able to fight off a threatened takeover bid, you may not get a reasoned response. You may instead find yourself at a baseball stadium. You look up and see the electronic scoreboard showing the home team behind by two in the eighth inning. Waking up, you may conclude that your efforts to fight the takeover can succeed, but the odds are against you and time is running out. (For further discussion of imagery and symbols of the subconscious, see Chapter Ten.)

Dreams also provide an effective way to counteract the excitement of the moment and to resist sales pitches that might look good but are really low and outside. Many people are experts at getting people to buy things they don't need— whether it's a new car for themselves or a new computer network for the company. Don't say yes until you sleep on it. On going to bed, ask the inner self to help you: "Do I really need this? Does the company really need this?"

Dreams are also useful in resolving moral questions. The dream-self—your real self—is the soul of conscience. It will always give you indications when you're doing something you shouldn't. Lady Macbeth's sleepwalking scene provides the most extreme example of dream admonition, but we've all been subject to it in one way or another.

It's advisable to heed these dream warnings, not because they're divinely inspired (they may or may not be), but because they come from yourself. They are warning letters that you've posted to your own electronic mailbox, and you sent them out of your deepest concern for what will make you happy.

In order to get the most help from your dreams, you need to learn how to invoke them, how to remember them, and how to keep track of them over a period of time. The three exercises that follow are designed with these objectives in mind.

Exercise: Creating a Bedtime Ritual

Deep dreaming takes place at the level of imaginative synthesis, or intuition; it is the free play of the magical child in its own element. Still, getting the subconscious to cooperate in the production and transmission of useful dreams can take a little doing. I've found that the inner child responds to a nightly ritual. When you go through certain habitual actions before bed, the intuitive part of you knows it's almost showtime, and it starts gearing up.

This bedtime ritual is a private affair, a secret agreement between your conscious and unconscious mind. There's no reason for it to be the same as anyone else's ritual. Whatever works for you is what you should do. Experiment with certain quiet, significant actions. Some people say a prayer each night. Others read from a favorite book. Still others run through a relaxation exercise and follow it with a set of affirmations of the sort suggested above.

All these approaches are good and will help get you into a receptive frame of mind. Once you have completed this part of the ritual, you're ready for the final step.

Set a small glass of clear water beside your bed. Tell yourself you are ready to experience significant dreaming. If you have a question you want answered in dream, ask it now. Ask it three times. In part, as we mentioned, the repetition will impress the question on the subconscious. But also, the triple statement of the question enforces the idea of ritual and incantation, as if you were calling on your own Delphic oracle. Then, slowly, drink a few sips of the water and go calmly to sleep.

When you wake up, drink several more sips of water, telling yourself that you will now remember the dreams you had. The ritual imbibing is yet another prompt for the subconscious to perform its wonders. The results are often dramatic.

Exercise: Dream Recall

First, train yourself to wake up at a certain time without the aid of an alarm clock or other disruptive sound. You can do it; just tell yourself, quietly and emphatically, when you intend to wake up. Within a week, you'll find your eyes opening at that time automatically. That permits you to have some calm, private moments when you first return to waking consciousness. Keep your eyes lightly closed, and stay "near the borderline" as long as you can, recalling as many dream images as possible.

If you feel you've just had an important and emotionally charged dream but can't quite remember it, do the following dream recall exercise:

Sink into a state of total relaxation. Imagine yourself alone in a movie theater. The number ten appears on the screen. The number is replaced by the main image of your dream. Sink deeper, say the number nine, and see a related image from the dream. Feel the number eight, and allow still other images from the dream to appear before your mind's eye. Sense the numbers seven, six, five, letting the dream's atmosphere and imagery collect once again around you. Four, three, two, one. You now clearly remember what the dream felt like, what you were doing in it, what you were wearing, what it all meant.

If you have a fast-starting morning, you might just jot down the main imagery of the dream on awakening, then rush off to do whatever you need to do. Later in the day, sit in a chair in a quiet place, look at your notes, and do the dream recall exercise just outlined. If it's an important dream, the basic imagery will be there and will gradually unfold as the countdown proceeds. You may not get all of it, but you'll pick up the flavor, and with it the lesson the dream has to teach. But try not to let too much time go by between the dream and the recall exercise. If you wait till the end of a long day at the office, you may find you have only a few disjointed memories left.

GERALD JACKSON

Exercise: The Dream Notebook

An essential aspect of dream exploration is the mapping of your progress over a period of time. This can be done by keeping a dream notebook and entering the main storyline, imagery, and emotion of your dreams each morning when you wake up.

The essential thing is to jot your notes quickly, perhaps in disjointed phrases or single words, before the evanescent experience evaporates. Even so, it can take as long as twenty minutes to half an hour, so allow yourself enough time. Do your writing before getting up, before putting out the dog or putting on the coffee. Otherwise, you'll lose the dream, just as you'd lose a story you've written on your computer if you didn't push the save button.

Some people say they can't remember their dreams. This may be because of a lack of systematic practice, compounded by the need to jump out of bed in the morning and get going. Or suppose you have a new baby and awaken at five or six in the morning to his or her cries. Whatever prophecies your dreaming mind was confecting for you seem utterly obliterated. This can be distressing, but it is usually a temporary situation. And if there's an important question about which you need special dream guidance, you may barter dream time with your spouse. You can say, "Honey, will you take the first baby shift tomorrow morning? I need the extra dream time to work on a business problem." It is at least a highly original excuse.

The important thing is to keep up your dream notebook every day. Make it as much a habit as brushing your teeth. I've been keeping dream diaries for more than fourteen years now, and the experience has been of profound help to me. It has made me more psychically sensitive, and it seems actually to stimulate my dreams, making them richer and more laden with significant imagery, as if the dream-generating inner self is encouraged by the efforts of the conscious mind to keep up with it.

Beside your notebook keep several pens. If you have only one and it runs dry, you may lose an irreplaceable vision while

112

you're searching through your desk drawers for something to write with. Some people also keep a small tape recorder by their bed. Speaking is faster than writing and so may help you preserve more of the dream. (Later you should transcribe the tape, so that you can see what you've got.) The trouble with a tape recorder, though, is that you have to speak out loud into it, and sometimes the sound of your voice will dissipate the dream.

I don't write down every dream I have, even if I could remember them all. Some dreams are obviously more important than others. You can tell by the feeling they leave you with, even more than by the imagery. An ill-digested pizza can give you the wildest images in the world, but they are likely to be jumbled and without a sense of meaning. A dream that leaves you feeling moved, or elated, or at the brink of some important discovery needs to be written down immediately. Later, you'll want to review it and ponder its implications.

Jotting down your dreams each morning provides three benefits: it stimulates the dreaming process (resulting in more and clearer dreams in the future); it improves your ability to recall your dreams with exactitude; and it provides a long-term context for judging the meaning of any given dream.

It is likely that over a month's period you will begin to see a pattern; you will be able to connect your dreams the way you'd connect points on a graph. Recurrent images will begin to stand out, similar themes, certain fears or fantasies. Your inner self may be trying to tell you something; it may be using a succession of related images in an effort to get through. Pay attention to these points of similarity.

Finally, keep in mind that every dream has a reason, and thus a message. Dreams reflect the life you are living, and if you consider them to be insignificant night after night, you may need to examine the quality of your waking life. If your dreams are frequently disturbed, confused, and upsetting, that may mean that your waking life is full of stress. Until you deal with that stress, you will not have clear, instructive dreams. If your dreams are frequently upsetting, you may have an emotional problem that is expressing itself through dreams. In that event,

113

a biofeedback specialist, or even a psychotherapist, could prove useful.

But whatever your dreams may be, seek always to learn their message. Don't be afraid of them, but sail on confidently. For better or worse, they represent the still, small voice of your own spirit, come to instruct you in the night.

10 Interpreting Your Own Symbols

Dreaming is easy, an effortless float down the subterranean river of consciousness. The hard part is knowing what to do about your dreams once you wake up.

The initial difficulty is remembering them at all. The houses, battles, joys, levitations, and emotional entanglements that seemed so real and engrossing while you were asleep quickly evaporate in the uncompromising light of day.

If you do remember the main feelings and images of your dream, then you get to the tricky part—figuring out what it all means. Many people, especially those who value sequential logic and sound common sense above all things, find dreams a daunting and unsettling subject. What do all these images, sounds, and emotions signify?

Before attempting to answer that, it might be helpful to consider for a moment the meaning of meaning. Does a Cubist collage by Picasso or Juan Gris "mean" anything? Certainly it *has* meanings; but a rapaciously logical approach to such a work may extort those meanings at the expense of the esthetic experience. A dream, like a painting, is first of all an experience. It is the work of the child artist, using the materials at hand. Most likely, those materials will consist of events, feelings, and impressions from waking life. A deep dream is an

115

imaginative reordering of those materials; and we view the dream, not as we look at an anagram or a telegram, to puzzle out meanings, but as we approach a work of art.

That may be why we so often wake up with a sense of pleasure, quickly followed by a feeling of regret as the dream begins slipping from memory. Our days begin with a farewell.

The message, or meaning, therefore, is only one aspect of the dream function. It is, however, the aspect that can most directly help us in our daily struggles and concerns, and so that's the part we tend to concentrate on. And often this is a proper approach, because some dreams are primarily message dreams, just as some paintings are propaganda art. They're not as deep as our more sublime visions, but they may be of more immediate use.

Sometimes meanings lie fairly close to the surface; i.e., they're expressed in terms that are similar to those we use in waking life. A woman executive, a client of mine, asked her subconscious for dream guidance as to whether or not she should go to Nashville on a business trip. She dreamed that she was on an airplane and that country western music was playing over the loudspeaker. It was not difficult for her, upon awakening, to connect the music with the town of Nashville, home of the Grand Ole Opry. Since the feeling of the dream was positive, she took it as an indication that she should go. Naturally, if she'd dreamed that the plane to Opryland ran into thick fog and began losing altitude, she might have considered staying home.

I've had some fairly literal dreams myself. Recently, I wasn't feeling up to my usually high level of energy. I asked for some guidance about this as I went to sleep, and I dreamed I was walking through a shopping mall. I came to a Chinese restaurant and saw a big black X over the door. It's hard to imagine how my subconscious could have made its message clearer. I cut out the Chinese food and felt immediately better.

Such literal messages are a rarity. The intuitive part of us does not use the one-to-one logic of daily consciousness. Its symbolism can be arcane, its methods associative and suggestive rather than direct. And most of the time its vocabulary

116

is imagastic rather than verbal. Dream interpretation is complicated by the fact that most people have muddled dreams to begin with. It can seem hopeless to try to extract guidance from a jumble of ill-remembered images. But be patient. The more you work with your dreams, writing down their main points and meditating on their meaning, the clearer they will become. They may still seem mysterious, but they will cease being chaotic. Most importantly, the *feeling* of the dream will come through more strongly.

Suppose, for instance, you ask for dream advice about a certain expansion opportunity you've been considering. The images you wake up with may seem at first unrelated to the subject, but the feeling of the dream is very positive, and you find yourself thinking about the expansion plans with more confidence than before. I would take that as a good sign. Later, with repeated practice, the symbolism of your dreams will begin to yield up its meanings; but those meanings will never contradict the underlying feeling you have woken up with.

Sometimes the imagery can be elaborate indeed, and may lead you on a merry chase. The dream that led me to my first literary agent is a good example of what I mean. Like many struggling authors, I was having trouble finding good representation, and so I decided to ask for help in a dream. I fell asleep with this request strongly in my mind and dreamed that I'd taken a plane to the island of St. Croix. I saw an Indian there, in feathers and full regalia, outside a fancy hotel. I passed him, went through the lobby and out to the hotel's pool, where I met a gray-haired man. He was the agent I was looking for.

On awakening, I followed my usual procedure, quickly writing down all the details of the dream that I could remember, including any emotions that I felt about the imagery or about the dream in general. One thing I had to decide was whether to take the dream literally or figuratively. Was I really supposed to pack up and fly to the Caribbean?

Over the next couple of days, I meditated several times about that question and concluded that, as far as possible, I should follow the scenario just as I had dreamed it. That was my gut feeling about it, my confirming intuition.

In interpreting any dream, I always ask myself what images particularly stand out. I realized that in this dream the Indian was very important. I got some travel brochures about St. Croix and went through them. Suddenly I saw the name Club Commanche and was convinced that the Indian was a clue to the hotel I was supposed to stay at. It felt right.

So I flew to St. Croix, checked in at the hotel, made my way to the pool. And right there, standing at poolside, was the gray-haired man from my dream! I struck up a conversation with him and asked him if he was a literary agent. As a matter of fact, he said, no, he wasn't. Why did I imagine he was?

When I told him about the dream, he was fascinated. He said that an upstairs neighbor of his, back in New York, had just published a book. He would send her a postcard suggesting that she get in touch with me.

A short time later, this New York author happened to see me being interviewed on Regis Philbin's TV program, "The Morning Show." That and the postcard from St. Croix prompted her to contact her agent about me. The agent then wrote to me and eventually signed me on.

It's a long way around the Caribbean to land a New York agent, but there it is. I followed my dream and the dream came true.

Several things about this whole experience are worth keeping in mind when it comes to interpreting your own dreams. First, I was given only as much information as I could use. Had the dream qualified its message, telling me that, no, the gray-haired man was not really the agent but would, in a roundabout way, lead me in the right direction, I might have woken up with a confused impression and would probably never have undertaken the trip to St. Croix. The dream, you might say, fibbed, in order to get me to act.

And that's another thing to keep in mind: dreams are not always accurate. It's not important that they should be, only that they get you moving in the right direction.

Also, the dream we're talking about had definite elements of clairvoyance, suggesting a creative presence behind it that borders on the omniscient. The gray-haired man by a hotel pool a thousand miles away was not someone I could possibly have known about. And when I met the man at the Club Commanche, I recognized his face from the dream.

A final point about this dream is that it used symbols and even visual puns to make its point. In the dream I'd seen an Indian, and I knew he was an important element. But I had no idea he was there as a sort of psychic logo for the hotel. It's amazing that the mind can perform such virtuoso gymnastics, and I can offer no explanation. I must leave that to the theologians and brain researchers. All I know is that it works.

I've also found that a dream image can mean two things at once, which can complicate your job of interpretation. To give a simple example, I was away from home working very hard, seven days a week, and during this time I dreamed that my little dog was neglected; her hair was matted and she had fleas.

When I got back home a few days later, I discovered that the person I'd hired to take care of my dog had not done her job. There was little Crystal, matted and full of fleas. I was devastated. But I also recognized that she was a symbol of my inner child; and after my marathon work period, I myself felt matted and neglected (no fleas, however). I had not been taking care of myself.

A more complex example of a double image appeared in a dream I had a few years ago, when I was trying to decide whether or not to leave Los Angeles. I dreamed that I was in a car with a friend and he drove the car off a cliff, killing both of us. On reflection, I realized that he'd been "steering" my career in the wrong direction, and that if I allowed him to continue the result would be disastrous. I left L.A. on the basis of that dream.

Four months later, my friend did have an accident in that car, and it involved the steering. He didn't go off a cliff, but the car was demolished. So the car imagery was both symbolic and literal, and the dream was a warning.

People tend to dream a lot about cars (or buses or trains), and frequently the image refers to the physical body, which is sometimes called the vehicle of the soul. Any car trouble in your dream should make you ask about the state of your health.

119

Cars often have a related meaning as well. They can symbolize the "direction" your life is taking and can tell you whether you're in the "driver's seat" or not. If you're in a bus and the president of your company is driving, you might ask yourself if you've given your power over to that person. If, on the other hand, your secretary is driving, you might conclude that you've got a personnel problem. Your secretary should not be steering your career.

A few years ago, I dreamed that I was driving my car downhill and the brakes didn't work. I'd been living in a social and professional whirl for some time before that, and I concluded that the dream was telling me to slow down. I cut back my schedule, did more relaxation exercises, and began feeling much more at peace.

A house is another image that frequently stands for the body. This truth was dramatically brought home to me a while ago when I had an illness that doctors seemed unable to diagnose. They tested me for mononucleosis, hepatitis, and everything else they could think of, but all they could say definitely was that I had an elevated white blood count, indicating a possible infection.

I asked for help from the subconscious, and that night I dreamed that I was in the kitchen of a house. Workmen were putting up new wallpaper and the appliances were all shiny, but I saw that the floor was caving in. I woke up alarmed, wrote down the imagery, and thought about it. The kitchen, I reasoned, is where you eat; so maybe it represented the mouth. The beautiful wallpaper and new appliances would then indicate that I had nice-looking teeth. But the floor was caving in. Maybe there was an infection in the bottom row of teeth or in the gums. I had an oral surgeon do X rays, and he discovered an impacted wisdom tooth which was abscessed and draining into my system. He operated on it and I felt entirely better.

A house in a dream does not always, of course, represent the body. Sometimes it represents a house. The meaning of dream imagery is largely determined by your preoccupations at the time you fall asleep. In my case, I had specifically asked for dream guidance about my health, so when I dreamed about a house I had good reason to suspect that the image referred to my body. If I had gone to sleep asking for guidance about real estate, that same dream might have suggested an entirely different interpretation. I might have been concerned that a property I was considering had a termite problem. So in interpreting any dream, even the most confusing, take into consideration the imagery, the underlying feeling, and just as importantly, the state of mind you were in when you fell asleep.

As we've seen, dreams can often help you with health problems—even when it seems the doctors cannot. They're particularly useful as early warning signs of stress-related illness. The kind of stress many executives experience can lead to a variety of health problems, from chronic headaches to peptic ulcers. But it takes a while, perhaps six months to a year, for stress to do its destructive work. You therefore have an opportunity to dream about a future illness in time to prevent it.

Stress dreams tend to have certain recognizable characteristics. The most extreme are usually dreams of falling, when you wake up with a jolt just before hitting bottom. In more subtle dreams, an underlying emotion of fear can signal hurry or stress. The imagery can also be a giveaway. You may dream that you're addressing a large audience and can't find your notes. You may find yourself onstage and you can't remember your lines. You may find yourself back in school taking an exam and knowing you're not prepared. You may find yourself naked in a crowded restaurant. Your dreams are telling you that you feel vulnerable, open to criticism, unable to meet the demands of your position. Often the people who have these dreams are doing just fine in their jobs, at least on the surface. But they may feel that they're really fooling people and that one day everyone will find out how incompetent they are.

If you have stress or anxiety dreams, take them as a warning to change your approach to your job and perhaps your approach to your personal life as well. Take a vacation. Do relaxation exercises. Build psychologically healthy relationships and terminate unhealthy ones. Remind yourself that business is a game and that, on some level, you're in it for the fun of it. If the anxiety dreams persist, maybe you're telling

121

yourself to change jobs. In any case, your dreams are presenting you with data that you can use to live a happier, more successful life. You ignore your dreams at your own peril.

Exercise: Seven Steps to Unlocking a Dream

1. Before you can decode your dream imagery, you need to remember it accurately. That's why it's so important to keep a dream diary of the sort we spoke of in the previous chapter. Keep a notebook and several pens beside your bed, and quickly scribble down everything you can remember about the dream, including the emotions that certain images aroused in you. Make a practice of recording your dreams every day; that will improve your facility in remembering them, and it also spurs the subconscious to generate further dreams.

2. After you've gotten the details down, ignore them for a moment and try to put the gist of your dream into one sentence, a sort of fortune-cookie version of the elaborate dream experience you've just gone through. This will help you zero in on what is most important. The sentence you write should include the basic contents of the dream and the feeling you came away with.

2A. Don't get lost in the imagery. This is a corollary to the point just made. You are trying to save, in two hands, an artifact that has the fragility of a snowflake. Don't handle it too much. See the images in relation to each other, however intriguing it may be to pursue one or another of them separately. Suppose you were allowed one minute to read a Shakespeare sonnet you'd never seen before and then it was taken away. If you fixed your attention on one striking phrase (say, "When time hath carved deep trenches in thy beauty's field"), you'd miss the flow and indeed the point of the whole poem.

3. Make a quick list, just ten or twelve words, of qualities that strike you about the dream. Allow yourself no more than thirty seconds to do it. The words may be adjectives, nouns, even verbs. The point is to cast onto the page perceptions that

may already be fading back into the subconscious. One or more of the words may surprise you. If you dream about a merry-go-round, for instance, it would be significant, as well as surprising and unlikely, if your quick list began: sunny, orange, child, smiling, death . . .

4. Determine the dominant words and images in the dream. Is it clear to you what they signify? If it's not, look them up in a dictionary, or even a thesaurus. Your subconscious may be working by association and connotation, rather than by denotation. If a pickle is an important image, does it mean you should eat more cucumbers? Does it mean you're *in* a pickle? Does it mean you should "marinate" more, mull things over, before acting? Does it mean you're pregnant?

5. If the dream feels important but you still don't know what it means, the next step is to do a meditation on it. Get yourself into a relaxed state, and count down very slowly from ten to one. See each number, one at a time, flashing on a movie screen in your mind, and feel yourself sinking more deeply into your essential, dream-making self each step of the way. When you are perfectly relaxed and in tune with yourself, gently pose questions about the dream. Visualize the primary images and feel the quality and the atmosphere that they evoke. In that lightly meditative state, the images will regain much of their original iridescence, just as shells do when you slip them back into the sea.

6. Don't tell many people about your dream or ask their advice about what an image means. Only a person extremely close to you can give you useful information about your dreams. The imagery is simply too personal. One man's pickle is not the same as another man's pickle. Nor does the dream-weaving inner self deal in clichés, except, perhaps, to give them an original twist. So the only way to determine the meaning of the images you meet in dreams is to use your intuition, test them on your pulse. With practice, and with the sense of continuity that a dream diary can give you, you'll begin to recognize recurrent image-clusters and understand what they signify in your life.

7. Finally, and most important, act on your dream. If you

have stress-filled, confusing dreams, your inner self is telling you to change the way you conduct your life. If you have a dream full of specific instructions (such as the dream I mentioned, through which I found my first agent), take a deep breath and follow those instructions.

If you're a dress manufacturer and you see a lot of children in your dream, you might consider expanding into children's clothing. Or maternity clothes. Such messages are especially worth heeding if they come in response to a specific request on your part for dream guidance about your career.

As you get more practice recording and analyzing your dreams, you will naturally become more confident of the wisdom inherent in them. Dreams will seem less confusing, more prophetic. But then you need to do something. Have the courage of your own creativity and take positive action. Dreams can provide you with warnings, urgings, inspirations—sometimes even a treasure map. But you have to mount the expedition yourself. Go forth to dig up the gold.

11 Color Scheming

In too many office spaces, dominated as they are by glass and steel, color is something one tends to think about every few years when the company's decorator comes around and asks if, this time, you want your office bright white or oyster white. Carpeting tends to be utilitarian—dark green or gray—and partitions generally favor beige. The philosophy, if it can be called that, seems to be that visual boredom is necessary for a productive work environment.

If you don't have a say in your company's choice of color scheme, so be it; you can provide your own touches of significant color in your own workspace. But if you do have some input in the decision, take the opportunity to shape the whole atmosphere and mood of the place by a judicious use of color.

We are all tremendously affected by color, often subliminally, without realizing it. The process is really quite mysterious. Color is not a thing; it is a continual event, an effect produced in the brain by careening light waves of different lengths and frequencies. There is nothing passive about the perception of color. Every time your eye alights on the red dictionary on the shelf above you, the light from that book stimulates the red color cones in the retina. Red light, having the longest wave length, travels more rapidly than, say, blue light, which has a shorter wave length. A red book with blue lettering would produce a virtual scrimmage of neurons. That may be good or bad, depending on the effect you want. Generally you want to surround yourself with colors that will help you, stimulating both productivity and intuition. And you want to avoid color combinations that present obstacles to clear thinking and clairvoyance.

The many physiological effects of color have been explored by scientists and discussed in laymen's terms in a number of useful books. In this chapter, though, we want to emphasize the effects that color can have on one's intuition. Colors provide an objective correlative to the subconscious mind, and they can often stimulate the intuitive faculty.

I've found that pink is a good color to surround yourself with when you're meditating. Its vibration helps you to focus, and it invites the subconscious to express itself. Of course, the color can pose a problem if you do some of your meditation exercises in the office. Unless you're Elizabeth Taylor, you might not be able to get away with painting your office pink. Very likely, you wouldn't want to. It's not a color that's easy to live with day in and day out; and anyway, your colleagues might start whispering about you around the water cooler.

Violet is also the color of intuition. Unfortunately, it is equally unsuitable as a dominant color for most office spaces. The solution is to accessorize your office with objects that contain your significant colors. You don't want business colleagues to feel that coming into your office is like entering Merlin's cave; your office should be as "executive-looking" as anyone else's. But you can easily create your own secret power zone where you do your meditating and inner communing. This zone can be powered up with, say, a violet-colored stone which doubles as a paperweight, or a pink blotter, or an abstract painting filled with colors that have a special meaning for you.

Your desk (if kept totally free of clutter) often makes a good power zone, or else a corner of the office where you have a chair and coffee table. What matters is that, when you close the door, you have an area you can go to that is your private altar to the inner self.

Probably the most noticeable touches of color in the workplace are to be found in the clothes people wear. It has been said that for the past several centuries people haven't been wearing clothes, they've been wearing costumes. There is a lot of truth to that. Certainly the air-conditioned lives we lead nowadays seldom require us to dress for physical survival. We dress for career survival. This generally means dressing conservatively, but using color to make subtle statements about who we are. A touch of yellow conveys the sense that the wearer is awake, bright, positive. Blue connotes calmness and approachability. A recent fad has been "power ties" for men. Mostly, these ties are red, sometimes yellow, usually silk, and they act like little visual affirmations: "I am powerful." And of course they deliver that same message about you to everyone you meet.

But messages change with the times. Another touch of red, the tip of a lit cigarette, used to be a way of saying, "I'm sophisticated, competent, important, and wrapped up in a cloud of creative thought." Symbolically, it was like carrying a weapon, a stick of fire. But now that cancer warnings have driven the well-informed and well-disciplined away, cigarettes are smoked most heavily by manual laborers and teenage girls. An executive who smokes heavily is now saying, "I am nervous, compulsive, inconsiderate, weak-willed, and, as an added bonus, I've got terrible breath."

A larger fire-stick, the cigar, has been even more vigorously banished from polite society, including from offices and restaurants and most other indoor spaces—with one significant exception. The real power man in the company, the original Mr. Gotrocks, the founder, the Mr. Big, is still seen puffing away on his beloved cigar. And in his case, the cigar is indeed a badge of his power; it is heraldic, proclaiming to the world that he has so completely arrived and is so confident of himself and so heedless of the opinion of others that he does not need to conform to the health fads of the masses. Of course, to get the right effect, it's essential that he puff a ridiculously expensive cigar, the sort one buys at the 21 Club, for instance, or a hand-rolled Finnish cigar. That way, the mega-executive conveys the added message that he has money to burn.

If red conveys an implication of firepower, forcefulness, and combustibility, other colors carry opposite connotations.

127

Dress in any way that makes you feel good, of course; but at the same time be aware of the effect that certain color choices are likely to have on others. If you decide to wear a brown suit when you make a presentation to the board of directors, you should understand that in so doing you are creating an obstacle to having yourself (and therefore your ideas) regarded as important. Brown, the color of dirt, does nothing to heighten or dramatize your presence. It suggests ordinariness rather than distinction. It's best worn by someone who wants to be thought a man of the people, a regular Joe, a plain nice guy, nothing special.

Gray, the traditional color of men's business suits, can be very spiffy, but it also conveys the message that you're not different from any other man-in-the-gray-flannel-suit. A subtle pattern or the addition of a bright accessory can help counteract that impression. And a fine, white-on-white striped shirt with French cuffs can heighten the elegance of the gray suit, creating an ensemble with a powerful effect. This is, of course, true only if the gray is a dark one (perhaps with a subtle stripe) and the material is obviously made of fine goods. Light gray makes men aesthetically invisible. It might be fine for company spies, who don't want to be remembered, but not for a man who wants to make an impression.

Since men generally have a limited choice (basically gray, blue, or brown) in their suits, I would go with blue whenever possible. It is a more positive color than the other two; it is alive and welcoming, while at the same time elegant, particularly if it's a dark rich blue.

Women, of course, can wear a wide range of colors and still look professional. You might say that what a man can get away with in a tie, a woman can get away with in her suit or dress. No businessman can come to work in a yellow suit; but a woman can. If she has the coloration to carry it off (a minimum of yellow in her skin tone), she could look quite terrific. And if she does have the wrong coloration for yellow, she can still wear it, as long as she blocks it from her face with an intervening color.

You will also want to choose your colors carefully when applying for a new position or asking for a raise. You are quite able to speak for yourself, but it doesn't hurt to realize that clothes oftentimes proclaim the man (or woman) before you get to say the first word.

If you want to convey integrity and trustworthiness, wear some combination of blue. The darker the blue, the more strength conveyed. You could, of course, go in with red, but such a proclamation of your own power might be perceived as a

Colors in the Executive Wardrobe

Color	Message	Clothing Tips
Red	Power	Draws attention. Can be intimidating. Use sparingly.
Orange	Spiritual joy	Not for business. Evokes negative reactions in our culture.
Pink	Love, warmth	Not for business, except fashion or cosmetics industry. Women should wear it, if at all, as an accessory, and in an icy shade.
Yellow	Intellect, alertness	Fine for accessories. Generally avoid if you have yellow skin tone.
Green	Calmness	Can be too soothing, even sleepy; use in accessories only.
Blue	Authority, trust, energy	Great as a dominant color for both men and women. Dark blue suggests trustworthiness, light blue suggests likability.
Indigo	Intensity, power	Accessories only.
Violet	Royalty, priestliness	Men: avoid. Women: accessorize sparingly with lavender shades.
Black	Great power, authority	As dominant color, commands respect. Fine for both men and women who want to be taken seriously.
White	Purity	It makes a positive statement if pristine; otherwise negative. Perfect for shirting and accessories.
Brown	Earth	Except in accessories such as shoes and handbag, avoid. Even then, the brown should be rich, dark.
Gray	Safe, conservative	As dominant color, commands respect, especially in dark shades.

threat to the person interviewing you. It's perhaps best to use small touches of red in such an instance—perhaps a blue tie with red stripes.

We may be talking psychology more than intuition here, but the line between them can be as thin as a pinstripe. After all, what you wear affects the subconscious perceptions of the person who sees you. Color reaches deep into the psyche, and even *thinking* about certain colors can affect your outlook and health.

Exercise: Color Cleansing

Find ten minutes of private time, and get yourself into a relaxed state (see deep breathing instructions at the end of Chapter One). The exercise which follows is both subtle and powerful. Give yourself time to feel each step as you go along. As with previous exercises, you may want to use your tape recorder and read the instructions into it. Then the voice instructing you will be your own.

Sitting straight in your chair, your eyes lightly closed, visualize the base of your spine. Feel the primal life force glowing red with energy at the end of the spinal column. It is a warm red light and you can feel its force infusing you with raw, elemental power.

Gradually, visualize your consciousness moving up to the genital region, where the light modulates to orange, the color of vitality and joy. As you feel that area of your body glowing orange you feel your sexuality and vitality growing stronger. Sexuality is a powerful, positive force in every aspect of your life, particularly when its manifestations are subtle and understated. You feel this force suffusing your genital area, creating a feeling of joyful capability throughout your whole body and spirit. There is nothing you cannot do.

Slowly, you move up to the solar plexus and the light modulates to yellow, the color of alertness and enthusiasm. You feel the yellow glow there in the network of nerves behind the stomach. Happiness effuses through your being.

And then, slowly, you move up to the heart, which is gradually filling with a soft green light, the healing, strengthening color of nature.

130

The heart is also the center of forgiveness, the healing of rifts between people. Feel the green light in the heart, knowing that to forgive others is to heal yourself.

Visualize your consciousness rising slowly up to your throat, as the light within you modulates to blue, the color of calmness and control. The words you speak from that energy center will be quietly authoritative, based in truth. Feel the blue in your throat.

Then, slowly, visualize the area just above the bridge of your nose and allow the light to modulate to indigo. This is where mystics say the "third eye" is located, the place within us from which we see the future clearly and the consequences of our decisions.

Finally, visualize the crown of your head, the jumping-off place of the spirit, and feel the pure, intuitive, violet light of that energy center.

Stay in that clear violet state for a minute or two, as long as you can feel it as a presence. Then gradually allow the colors to fade as you return to your daily consciousness. You are returning cleansed, more focused, refreshed.

When you are ready, open your eyes. The world you see may appear saturated with color, because you are more sensitive to colors now, and to their various emotional resonances.

Exercise: Quick Fixes

Meditating on certain colors can actually be therapeutic, helping you with difficulties you may face during the day. Again, get yourself into a relaxed state and allow your mind to empty of worries and sequential thought.

If you suffer from *low energy* today, if the baby kept you up or a deadline made you lose sleep, meditate on the color red. Don't think, just see, feel the warm power of redness. It will give you an influx of energy.

If you have a *headache,* and you're so nervous you feel like jumping out the window, meditate on ice blue. Allow the coolness of it to fill your mind. Hold that feeling as long as you can. It will calm you down, and you'll find that the headache has lessened or disappeared entirely.

If you don't feel creative today, if you *need inspiration,* give yourself a psychic kick in the pants by meditating on the

131

color yellow. It's perhaps no accident that kids in grade school are given yellow pads and bright yellow-coated pencils. It signals the mind to be alert.

If you want to get quickly into the *intuitive frame of mind,* visualize bubblegum pink. Let your mind float in that warm, mild color, without any specific thought. It's a warm bubble bath for the mind, fun and cleansing at the same time. The subconscious tends to respond to this easy color, as a child might respond to an invitation to come out and play on a warm afternoon.

And for city-dwellers, or for anyone suffering the *depressive effects of nature deprivation,* meditate on a rich, living green.

In fact, I'd suggest going beyond meditation and actually getting some green plants in your office. Not only is the color spiritually healing, the plants themselves can absorb polluting chemicals as part of the photosynthetic process. "If you put plants in buildings, will it help improve air quality?" asked Dr. B. C. Wolverton, the NASA investigator in charge of plant research, in a recent *New York Times* interview. "We say, from our tests, yes indeed. The more foliage, the healthier the environment is going to be."

Recent NASA research suggests that the gerbera daisy and the chrysanthemum are able to filter benzene (a carcinogen) out of the air. The philodendron and golden pothos can help remove both benzene and carbon monoxide. Aloe vera has proved effective in removing low concentrations of formaldehyde.

Dr. Wolverton of NASA has applied his findings to his own home environment. He built a solarium and filled it with palms, golden pothos, philodendron and other therapeutic plants; then he modified the ventilation system so that the air in his house would be continually drawn through the solarium. It is an experiment that corporations might do well to look into, when it comes time to remodel or relocate. As many as 90 percent of office buildings, according to recent reports, have inadequate or nonexistent ventilation. The effect on employee energy level is extremely detrimental. If the importing of green plants can help raise energy, brighten spirits, and reduce the number of sick days, it might prove cost-effective.

Imagine the effects that such an innovation could have. First, there'd be the healing sight of the solarium, which should be visible from as many parts of the building as possible. Benches would be provided, and employees would be welcome to stroll through the solarium on their lunch hour, soothing their eyes with a panoply of colors. Then there is the improvement and enlivening of the air—the fresh scent of growing things filtering through the air vents. And finally, there is the substantial reduction of industrial pollutants—the curse of many if not most office buildings in operation today.

No doubt about it, the greening of the American workplace is an idea whose time has come.

12 Getting the Timing Right

$\mathbf{A}$s wonderful as it is to have flashes of intuition, it is not enough. You also need to know the time-frame to which they apply. You may, for example, have a strong intuition that gold is going to reach $1,400 an ounce, but it would be wise to hold off investing in the gold market until you had some idea when this remarkable price level will be reached. If you know it's going to happen next month, then don't delay; if it's happening in A.D. 2009, you have time to look into a CD or two first.

Timing is everything in the stock and bond markets, and it's essential to almost every business, from real estate to the rare book trade. And yet, timing is the trickiest part of ESP. Even the best psychics are sometimes off in their timing. I wish it were otherwise.

It's not hard to see why this might be so. The right side of the brain, which is used for spatial and intuitive functions, among others, is not the center which is concerned about time. It's common to hear of a creative artist, in the throes of his work, looking out the window in surprise to find that it is already nightfall. "The hours flew by," he may say. Or, "I lost all track of time." That's what happens to every one of us when we sleep. The dreams may seem to go on forever, or they may seem to fly past, but dream time is never anything like eastern

134

standard time. You may dream *about* time, as Alice dreamed of the time-obsessed White Rabbit, but while you're in Wonderland you probably won't know what time it is.

But that doesn't mean you can't find out. If you're in a state of meditation and receive a strong impression about an upcoming event affecting your business, force yourself to visualize a calendar. What month is it? Is it this year or next? Or visualize yourself looking out the window. Are the trees turning color? Are they covered with snow? Or are the heavy leaves gasping in summer heat?

I know it sounds a bit fantastic, the idea of shaping your visions while you're having them. It's almost like editing a movie while it's still in the camera—a tricky business, but not impossible. Don't expect to be wholly successful on your first try, however. Your priority is to get the psychic images flowing; only gradually, with patience and practice, will you begin to find ways to "massage" those images.

As you become adept at slipping into and out of the light, conscious trance state we call meditation, you may try yet another timing technique. Imagine yourself at a baseball stadium or at a basketball game (whatever your favorite game is). Look at the scoreboard. What time and date is lit up? Or visualize yourself walking in Times Square in New York City and looking up at the news headlines circling above you in lights. The answer to your question about timing is up there. All you have to do is read what it says.

In short, there may be no time, per se, on the psychic level, but there are images from which time can be inferred. You need to find the method that is most congenial to your own "subby," as I call the subconscious self. Let your subby tell you the answers you seek in the image system that he or she most enjoys using.

Do the same with your nighttime dreams. Before going to bed, ask for the information you need—whatever business question is on your mind—but also ask for an indication of the best business timing. You may or may not get an answer, but it's important to put the question. You might even project a visualization of yourself presenting your subconscious child with an imaginary Mickey Mouse watch. Ask him or her to show you the big and little hands so that you'll know when an intuited event is going to take place. Or visualize a desk calendar, if the time frame is longer than a day. Presenting the subconscious with a challenge can often lead to an ingenious response.

In any case, in the matter of timing, it's essential to put yourself through a rigorous period of psychic training before actually putting money on the line. And even when you get fairly good at timing your investments, job switches, expansions, or takeover defenses, I would still advise hedging your bets. The key to investments is diversification, and in the event your timing on pork belly futures is off, you'll still have your diamond mines in Secaucus.

Timing gets better the more you practice, just as the body gets stronger the more you exercise. I meditate for twenty minutes twice a day, which is one reason my intuitions are usually more accurate than those of people who meditate once a month. I keep a detailed dream diary, and before going to bed, I frequently ask the subconscious for help.

Exercise: Timing Practice

Use the basic relaxation techniques from Chapter One, getting into a state of calmness, then count down slowly from ten to one, sinking more deeply into your subconscious with each count. When you feel yourself to be in a condition of relaxed connectedness, invite the subconscious to answer the following timing questions. Even if you get just a vague feeling, take note of it and write it down.

1. Someone you know, perhaps a colleague, is expecting a baby. Imagine that you are looking at the birth announcement. What is the date on it?

2. Look in the paper and check the price of gold. On what date will the price of gold be ten or more dollars higher than it is today?

3. You are expecting a letter or check in the mail. Will it arrive this week? What day of the week will it be delivered?

4. A close relative will call you on the phone. When will the call come?

5. You're planning to watch a ball game tonight. If baseball, in what inning will the most runs be scored? If football, in what quarter will the most points be scored?

6. Think ahead to next week's action on the New York Stock Exchange. On what day will the Dow end at the lowest level for the week?

7. On which day will the Dow close at the week's highest level?

8. You have an important lunch meeting coming up. Ask your subconscious to tell you when the other person will show up. Will the person be late? Early?

9. A meeting has been called and you're expected to attend. At precisely what time will the meeting start? At precisely what time will it be adjourned?

10. When will you be given the next compliment?

What you are doing through exercises such as these is training your subconscious to "ride easy in harness," as Robert Frost once wrote about using strict poetic meters. The horses of the subconscious love to run free, but they can get used to a structure, even to a rudimentary sense of time, as long as it is made into a pleasurable activity.

There are other ways of determining the right time for a business activity, too. One method is the use of a pendulum, which is discussed in some detail in the next chapter.

Still another method is to consult the experience of psychics through history. They have generally found, for example, that around the time of the full moon emotions run high. Knowing this tendency, you may want to be a guard against being carried away by someone's sales pitch during that timeperiod; but you can also use this information to touch the emotions of others and make your own sales pitches more effective. The full moon is a great time for staging a publicity event, for example, or having a press party, or sending out press releases. You are likely to generate excitement and get maximum exposure.

137

Another bit of moon lore is that seeds planted between the full moon and the new moon (during the "waning" moon) tend not to grow well. But seeds planted between the new and the full moon (during the "waxing" moon) tend to come to fruition. So if you're launching a new product or a new campaign, or a new business, try to do it under the new moon. I wouldn't attempt to explain how or why this should work, but it generally does. Just try it, as a game, and see if it works for you.

Psychics also say that the best time to give up bad habits, or to kill weeds, or to get rid of troublesome clients, is during the last three days of the old moon—during "the dark of the moon"—before the new moon appears. This is the time for losing things, for ending business connections, not for initiating new projects. Pick up a copy of *The Old Farmer's Almanac* and check out when the phases of the moon will occur in your area. Such astronomical observations are not the only factor to consider, of course, when it comes to timing; but sometimes the best method is a combination of methods. It is one more tool giving you an edge in your business dealings.

Another important aspect of timing has to do with your own cycles and rhythms—what are called "biorhythms." You may at some point want to consult a biorhythm expert to explore this subject further; but you can also learn a lot on your own, by keeping track of the times when you are most and least energetic, most and least creative, etc. Mark these cycles on a calendar or in a notebook and look back to see if a pattern emerges. You probably know by now if you are a morning or a night person, and when during the day you tend to get the most work done. Do the same for the week and the month.

I have found, through my own unscientific observations, that women tend to be more intuitive just before their periods. That doesn't mean that they are not intuitive at other times of the month, or that the hunches they get before their periods are necessarily correct. They may, in fact, be incorrect, because ESP can be distorted by emotions, and emotions tend to run high during this time. But it's another factor to keep in mind when charting the ups and downs of your ESP manifestations.

With something as tricky as timing, it's advisable to bring

all your powers to bear on the problem—your intellect as well as your intuition—and to check one part of the mind against another. During the early 1980s, there were billions to be made in the video industry; but toward the end of the decade the industry entered a period of shakeout. Intuition, guided and checked by common sense, might have prompted you to invest in that industry in its early stages and warned you to bail out before the market became glutted. People made millions in commodities during the drought of 1988, by betting that it was going to get worse. There is no tragedy short of nuclear war that will not turn a profit for someone who has a hunch and then drives ahead and acts.

I personally feel that, with the graying of America, there will be a huge service industry in the '90s centered on taking care of old people in the home. The well-off elderly, who don't want to and don't have to go into nursing homes, will need people for shopping, cleaning, gardening, nursing. The timing is right for someone to come along and organize all these services into a one-stop, nationwide organization.

The same is going to be true of the day-care industry. It is presently in a sad, in fact intolerable, state; but with two-paycheck households becoming the norm, sheer social and economic pressures are going to cause day care to be reinvented during the 1990s, in the sense that McDonald's reinvented the hamburger. It's going to be streamlined, inexpensive, and franchised nationally.

Am I expressing intuitions here, or merely consulting my common sense?

Two magnificent writers in the early twentieth century had nearly opposite ways of understanding reality. One, André Gide, would pick up the object he wanted to understand, and he would scrutinize it from all angles under a strong light. But when his friend, the visionary German poet, Rainer Maria Rilke, wanted to understand something, he would close his eyes. To thrive in the complex business environment of the coming century, we need a bit of both approaches: eyes closed in meditation, eyes open in analysis.

This dual approach is particularly important for the increasingly large number of successful executives who are thinking of switching careers in midstream. In fact, unlike the last generation, most of today's executives change jobs regularly, as a way to advance. If this is your situation, you are probably already asking: "When is the best time to quit my job and jump to a new one?" Is it your plan to switch from one company to another, or do you want to go out on your own and be your own boss?

Faced with such prospects, you may feel as if you're at the edge of a ravine getting up the nerve to jump to the other side. Never has it seemed so important to see all aspects of the situation clearly.

First, I would suggest meditating about it several times, over a period of weeks. Determine your own motivations. Are you feeling a mid-life itch, intimations of mortality, boredom with your present routine, lack of challenge, personality conflicts with your boss, an uncomfortable level of stress?

Then, while still in meditation, consult yourself as to whether there's anything you can do to solve these problems without leaving your present job. If you are under a lot of stress, maybe you need to take a vacation and think about your situation from an emotional distance.

In general, don't quit to leave a problem; wherever you go there will be problems, maybe the same problems. Never quit in disgust. Wait until you're in a great mood, and then leave only if you're going to something dramatically better.

And don't romanticize the life of an entrepreneur. Do a thorough visualization on the life you'll be leading when you're your own boss. Do you really want to do the books? Do you want to have to take on the headaches of having employees?

If all your introspection leads you back to the conclusion that, yes, you must leave the old company, then the question becomes simply one of timing.

The answer to that question is that you'll *know* when the time is right. When your dreams tell you, and your intuitions tell you, and your logic tells you, and the arithmetic tells you, then it is time. Only then are all systems go. I have never seen anyone fail who had the desire, the determination, and the timing. And I've never seen anyone succeed who lacked these things.

So you do it. You take the leap. There's nothing in the world like the surge of power and excitement that comes with the knowledge that you are acting boldly and at exactly the right moment. *Carpe diem,* saith the sage; seize the day. All the fears that have been whispering to you up until that moment become suddenly inaudible in the rush of your life's acceleration. You're out there in the blue, "riding on a smile and a shoeshine," as Arthur Miller once wrote. That's when you really begin relying on your intuitions, your street smarts, whatever you want to call them.

And that's when you realize what a powerful resource they are.

13 Double-Checking Your ESP

In the course of developing the intuition, the important thing is to keep encouraging the part of the psyche we've been calling the inner child, or the subconscious. For this reason, it is natural to emphasize the successful product lines or ad campaigns and not to dwell on the duds. At the same time, though, you want to avoid falling prey to the Zagarnek effect.

Named after the psychological researcher, Charlotte Zagarnek, the effect in question describes the human tendency to remember one's successes and to forget one's failures. It is undoubtedly an important psychological defense mechanism against despair and discouragement, but it can be a danger if you want to keep an accurate record of how well you're doing.

To double-check the accuracy of your intuition, I suggest a five-step approach:

1. Test yourself frequently in small ways. That means practicing your ESP a lot, using trivial questions that have easily verifiable answers.

2. Run problems past the subconscious a second or a third time, using dreams and meditation techniques.

3. Check your answers by using a pendulum.

4. Do the market research and look at past business curves to give yourself a "reality check."

5. Examine your own motives and moods to detect any "spin" you may be putting on your perceptions.

Let's look at these one at a time. First, of course, you want to heed the advice of the man who was stopped on the street and asked how to get to Carnegie Hall. "Practice, practice, practice," he said.

This means taking every opportunity to intuit answers to small questions you have every day. Don't indulge in random guessing, however; talking off the top of your head won't help you become more intuitive. On the other hand, you don't always have to go through a long meditation exercise, either, before expressing a feeling about something. Try *throwing* yourself into an intuitive frame of mind. Clark Kent didn't need a dressing room and a valet in order to turn into Superman; after a while, all he needed was a second or two in a phone booth.

Here is a method that works for me: Close your eyes a few seconds and take three deep breaths, focusing your attention on a spot just above the bridge of your nose, the place that Eastern religions refer to as the "third eye." Then quietly ask yourself the question you want answered.

Feel free, however, to devise your own method for getting into the intuitive state quickly. This is, after all, your own secret place, and a private ritual may work better than anything you can get from a book. Some people visualize a calming color or think of a prayer or murmur a private mantra. Experiment with various approaches; and don't hesitate to ask yourself, when you are in the meditative state, what is the quickest way of getting there again. Your subconscious may suggest a word or an image for you to concentrate on, for the next time. That image may work the way a weight does for a diver, helping you descend quickly and touch bottom.

Actors do this all the time, to help throw themselves into a role. When Jack Lemmon was filming *The China Syndrome,* the producer, Michael Douglas, would hear him mumbling something to himself just before a scene started. As Douglas told the story at a recent awards ceremony, the mumbling went on before every take. Curious, Douglas moved closer, trying to catch the great actor's words. Finally, he heard what Lemmon had been whispering: "Magic time!"

Once you've found a shortcut that helps snap you into the intuitive zone, you can turn for practice to whatever questions happen to come up. It might also be a good idea to go back and redo "The One-Day Game" and "The Next Time Game" in Chapter Three, or the "Timing Practice" in Chapter Twelve. If you're planning to go on vacation in the Bahamas or in Las Vegas, you might try your fledgling talents out at the gaming tables—keeping your bets on the low side. With practice, you should at least win the office pool for the Super Bowl.

A second way to keep tabs on the accuracy of your intuitions is to do a remeditation or a redreaming about questions you've already asked for psychic help on. If you get similar answers a second time, you can feel more confidence that you were on the right track. If, for instance, you've been offered the chance to head up the company's new regional office in Detroit, you may have asked for dream guidance and come up with disturbing images of dirty snow, clogged evening traffic, and teenagers stealing the front left tire from your car. You've concluded that maybe Detroit is not for you.

So you ask again a week later. This time you see your company's Detroit office crumbling into the icy river. Different response, same message: Don't go.

A third way to double-check your intuition is by use of a pendulum. This may sound rather far out and New Age-y, but the principle is much the same as that of the dousing rod, which has been used for centuries to find water underground. The dousing rod is a flexible, forked switch of wood (often willow), and is held in two hands; the pendulum is a small object suspended on a chain, and is held in one hand. In both cases the object you are holding shows an alarming tendency to move of its own accord. The dousing rod dips irresistibly downward when it "senses" water beneath the ground, while the pendulum begins moving either sideways or up and down in response to a spoken or even an unspoken question.

In my experience, it doesn't seem to matter what the pendulum is made of. Some people insist that a small ball of crystal at the end of a thin gold chain gives the best results; but I've seen small gold crosses, silver Stars of David, even a steel peace sign work well, too. What counts is that the object be of some personal significance to the person using it. This suggests to me that the operative force is not some world-embracing electromagnetic current, but the action of one's own subconscious mind. I believe the pendulum is so effective because it is really just your inner child communicating with you.

Exercise: Using the Pendulum

Using a ruler, draw a cross on a piece of paper. Make the lines about four inches long and as close to right angles as possible. Determine where north is and sit so that you're facing in that direction, with the paper on a flat surface in front of you.

Before you ask a question, be sure it is phrased in a precise way and can be answered with a yes or no. It's not enough to ask if the price of silver will be going up. Of course it will, and it will be going down, too, given enough time. Ask if the price of silver in the U.S. will rise in the next two weeks.

Now, holding your hand very still, suspend the pendulum by its chain directly above the center of the cross. If the pendulum begins moving sideways (east and west), the answer to your question is no. If the pendulum moves vertically (north and south), the answer is yes.

Sometimes you can get a good reading without using the cross on the paper. If, for instance, you're deciding between several different properties to buy, lay the photo or floor plan of one of them on the table and hold the pendulum above it, asking, "Is this the property I should buy?" After you get an answer, lay down the picture of the next property and ask the same question.

In determining the timing of a purchase or of a contract signing, you might hold the pendulum over a week-at-a-glance calendar and ask, "Is this the week I should make this transaction?" If the answer is negative, turn the page to the next week and ask again.

In all of these experiments, the best approach is one of open-minded curiosity. A spirit of play is much more efficacious than an earnest effort to believe, or for that matter a stubborn determination to disbelieve. I've found that the pendulum doesn't always work with strong-willed people, because their conscious desires overpower the delicate actions of the subconscious self. You cannot will a psychic experience, any more than you can will a sexual experience.

Practice using the pendulum on minor questions, ones about which you can get outside confirmation within a few days. And do it often. Just as a child needs time to develop mind-body coordination, so you need time and practice to develop mind-mind coordination, or right brain/left brain coordination.

While you are exploring the above methods for double-checking your hunches, do not omit the mundane methods of market research, focus groups, comparison of notes with colleagues—the plain footwork that you've always relied on in the past. If, for instance, you have an intuition, or a dream image, or a pendulum indication that your surfboard company should move its headquarters to Alaska, it might be a good idea to do a "reality check" by looking at the research on surfboard sales in that part of the country.

And if, after all this, you still find yourself confused by mixed messages—a definite go-ahead from one source of information, an absolutely no from another—it may be a good idea to take the problem to a reputable psychic, someone whose track record is known to be good. (Consult the list of organizations in the Appendix to this book.) This is not an admission of failure on your part, but only a recognition that you are still learning and may not yet know how to read all the signs.

The point is not to take the psychic consultant's judgment as gospel, but to compare it with the information you already have. Then you must weigh the evidence and, using your own intuition yet again, come to a decision.

The final "reality check" is an honest introspection concerning your own motivations. The truth is, you will not get a true reading from any of the methods in this book if on some level you do not want the truth to come out. It is easy to sabotage yourself without ever being consciously aware of what you are doing. If you ask a question with a definite preference for one answer over another, for example, the pendulum can be turned into a psychic "yes man," telling you what you want to hear. In the long run, that means you're getting unreliable information.

It is because of this human tendency to put a "spin" on the truth, making it conform to one's desires, that I've come to consider detachment one of the most important qualities for a psychic. By this I don't mean indifference or vagueness, but nonattachment to *results*. Such a feeling runs counter to the prevailing get-me-results attitude of the business world; but in the long run it is exactly what the business world needs. No one can paint an inspired canvas if he's grimly determined to produce a masterpiece. No one can be intuitive who is determined to wring every marketable idea out of the subconscious. No one can learn the truth if he knows what answer he wants.

All the great religions and philosophies have been telling us this. Christian acceptance, Socratic admission of ignorance, Eastern abnegation, Judaic submission, all imply the same wisdom, that the way to happiness is to let go of preconceived ideas. Only then are you open to ideas and experiences that you've never conceived of before, perhaps even to divine inspiration. That's as much a prescription for business success as it is for getting into Heaven.

As Krishna (the higher self) tells Prince Arjuna in the ancient Hindu text, the *Bhagavad-Gita:* "He who abandons the desire to see a reward for his actions is free, contented. . . . When a man, so living, centers his heart in the true self and is exempt from attachment to all desires, he has attained to wisdom."

THREE

Managing People Through Intuition

14 Improving the Office Atmosphere

Every office you walk into has its own intangible feeling, and the more intuitive you become the more precisely you can define what that feeling or atmosphere is, and what it means about working conditions there.

Decor plays a role in such perceptions, of course. If the place is a windowless warehouse with exposed pipes and peeling paint, you're not likely to want to work there. But the atmosphere of a place goes deeper than a paint job. Indeed, there are many offices that look attractive but feel repellent, although you'd be hard pressed to say just why. There are lively offices and deadly offices. Which sort do you work in?

The truth is, you may not know. Sometimes daily routine dulls the critical faculties, and you may take the quality of life in your company for granted until you walk into another company's offices and feel the difference. That is a very good thing to do, incidentally. Then come back, solicit the opinions and suggestions of your own people, and do a private meditation on the work atmosphere in the home office.

Exercise: Making a Psychic Evaluation

The best way to take a reading on the working atmosphere in your company is to do a meditation on it. First,

151

relax your mind completely. Then go through the countdown exercise from Chapter Two and get into your level, into the feeling of being in contact with your subconscious self. You may be able to speed this process by taking three deep, cleansing breaths while keeping your mind concentrated on a point about an inch above the bridge of your nose.

This exercise really involves two meditations. For the first, ask yourself for some intuitions about the *physical* aspects of the office setup. Make a list of these questions beforehand.

You may, for example, ask yourself if the lighting is too harsh. Too dim? Just right? What can you do to improve it? (Often, replacing fluorescent lights with full spectrum bulbs can provide great relief for office workers.)

Are the computers user-friendly? Is there a headache-causing glare from the monitor screen? (Often, a glare-reducing mesh can be purchased, or the room's lighting source relocated.)

What is your intuition about the color scheme of the place? (See Chapter Eleven for a further discussion of this subject.) Is the carpeting depressing or enlivening? Is there bright and well-framed artwork on the walls?

Are there any live plants, and are they well cared for? The droop factor in office plants is sometimes a pretty good symbolic gauge of the energy level of the company.

Is the place kept clean? "Creative chaos" may work in some contexts, but an outfit that doesn't keep the halls vacuumed and waste baskets emptied is giving its workers a dual message: "Slovenliness is company policy," and, "We don't care about you."

Is there a "noise pollution" problem—whether from Muzak or machinery or outside street sounds? (You may need to put in soundproofing.) Are the desks too close together for privacy? Are there proper partitions between workspaces? Is the traffic pattern bad in the office? Are people getting in one another's way?

Do you suspect that you're working in a sick building, one in which chemicals are seeping into the atmosphere and causing health problems? How effective is the ventilation system? When was it last cleaned?

Go over all the physical aspects of the office layout and decor that you can think of. When you've gotten as many hunches, feelings, or images as possible about them, gradually relinquish the meditative state and return to your daily consciousness. Then quickly write down whatever you can remember and use these hints as springboards for some solid left-brained analysis. This is a good point to canvas the opinions and perceptions of others who work in the office.

In the next meditation session, go on to a consideration of *psychological* factors which may be affecting the work atmosphere.

Ask yourself first, Is quality work being done? What departments are working most effectively? Least effectively? Could this be in any way a result of the office atmosphere?

Is the office a friendly place? Or is it filled with stress, or inertia, or paranoia?

Is there a problem with absenteeism? Do people tend to come down with the flu on Fridays and Mondays?

Are people counting the minutes until they can leave for the day? Is the elevator jammed at 5:01 P.M.? If so, why do you think that is? Is it more true of one department than of another? What is the energy level in various parts of the company? Is it just that the people happen to be more energetic and self-motivated in one sector of the company, or do their supervisors treat them differently and create a different work atmosphere?

Is there a problem with office sabotage? With filching of pens, staplers, or other office equipment? To what extent? In what departments? And why?

Are your people loyal to the company? Do they see it as a place to stay and make a career? Or do people generally leave after a couple of years? What is your intuition about why this is so?

Finally, what do people think of you? Do they feel comfortable around you? Do they tell you the truth? Or do they keep things from you? What is your attitude toward them, and how does that attitude affect the work atmosphere in the office?

That's more than enough to ask your subconscious about for now. When you come out of your meditation, quickly jot down any thoughts, images, or impressions that you have, no

153

matter how illogical they may seem. Later, analyze these notes
for the hints they may contain.

STRIKING A BALANCE

There are all kinds of companies, of course, from
small entrepreneurial operations, involving perhaps yourself
and two or three others, to corporations employing thousands
of people. But in almost all cases, the office atmosphere is
determined by the boss. Whether by acts of omission or commission, she or he sets the tone.

My own view, after counseling many executives from all
sorts of companies, is that the ancient Greek rule of modera-
tion or balance should apply. If you're aloof, frosty, or dic-
tatorial, you'll create a fearful and resentful workplace. If you
are everybody's pal and avoid issuing directives for fear of
hurting people's feelings, you're creating an atmosphere of
confusion and indolence. This much is obvious. The hard part
is to find the balance between authority and authoritarianism,
between having control and being controlling, between being
the boss and acting bossy. It's a balance each executive must
strike intuitively. That's why it's important to do regular meditation exercises, tapping into the part of you that has the
answers and is honest enough to tell you the truth, whether you
want to hear it or not.

To take a hypothetical example, suppose that you are now
the COO (chief operating officer) of the company and that you
had to work your way up through miserable office environments for years, places where the boss was remote and the
main form of communication was rumor. You now have a
choice. You may resolve to overhaul the old organizational
model and open up communication channels with the workers.
Or you may unthinkingly fall into what is known as the hazing
syndrome: "I went through it, so you're going to have to go
through it, too."

No one is completely free from destructive behavior patterns, but an honest communing with your subjective self will

help you see what your particular syndrome may be and how it is affecting morale. The fact that you're reading this book suggests that you're more interested in moving into the future than in perpetuating the past. Your increasingly accurate intuitions will help you devise ways of breaking free of old patterns. What follow are a few suggestions. You will no doubt discover others to fit your particular business context.

CREATING AN OASIS

It has been shown that people who are relaxed and alert produce better quality work than people who are tired and upset. If your meditations reveal to you the existence of morale problems in the office, you need to look at ways to give a psychic vitamin B-12 shot to your employees—and to yourself as well. One way is to mold an aesthetically pleasing environment that lowers the stress level while raising the energy level. That means creating an office oasis, a place where employees can not only take a coffee break, but perhaps even a meditation break at the same time.

There are various ways this can be done. One media company I know has a small meditation room with dim, softly colored lights and oversize pillows on the floor. Any employee can go in there at any time and "cool out." The same company employs a masseur who comes around once a day and gives neck and shoulder rubs to anyone who wants them. The workers love these little attentions, not only because they help reduce stress, but also because they show that the company cares about them.

You might build on this idea, teaching interested workers some of the basic meditation techniques that are offered in this book. That way, their private time in the meditation room might be used not for a snooze, but for an energizing contact with their inner child.

The key to any such innovation is to emphasize its voluntary nature. Workers have enough obligations in their jobs without being *forced* to relax. For some people, too, words like "intuition" and "meditation" are suspect, suggestive of tarot cards and love crystals; so it might be well to describe the exercises as stress reduction techniques, or use some other easily acceptable label.

In the same spirit, paint the coffee room or office kitchen a relaxing, meditative color (a soft pink?), and put in some plants and fish tanks. Watching fish is relaxing and can actually lower one's blood pressure and heart rate. It also tends to put people into an alpha mode, which is the intuitive, right-brained state of mind. But there's no need to use that terminology. Just say you've found this wonderful, wacky new interior decorator.

It's a good idea to install an ionizer as well, so that people will be breathing charged-up air. And instead of Muzak, why not put in quiet tapes of ocean murmurs or other calming natural sounds. If you choose music, baroque is best—something mathematical and abstract—or else a New Age composer such as Vangelis or William Ackerman or Andreas Vollenweider.

You'll want to designate a smoking room that is separate from the kitchen area we've been describing. Smoke and alpha waves don't mix, quite apart from the other unfortunate side effects of smoking. But smokers need to feel included in the company, too, and their area should be pleasant and (especially) well-ventilated.

While you're creating coffee-break areas and meditation chambers, you might think of setting aside a room for exercising. We're not talking about lockers and Jacuzzis here, just a carpeted room where employees can loosen their ties and do a few calisthenics or yoga exercises. The idea is not to work up a sweat, but to get the blood aerated and to help people get in touch with their bodies.

Again, such activity must be voluntary to be effective. It should be led by a reputable exercise or yoga consultant, and might best be offered twice a day, the second time in mid-afternoon, when workers' energy tends to be low.

Such office oases provide workers with crucial psychological safety valves, and the expense of setting them up is gener-

156

ally far outweighed by improved morale and increased productivity.

The prime determinant of office morale, however, remains the relationship of the boss to those who work under him. The meditations you have been doing will give you a pretty accurate reading of the office dynamics and should therefore help improve your management approach. But you need also to institute a system of incentives that will make people feel encouraged and included.

That means asking their opinions and making it safe for them to give an honest response. Too often, the CEO is the last to know.

It means making sure that everyone, from the typist down the hall to the executive vice president of the company, has a clear idea of his or her job description. The truth is that most workers don't know exactly what they were hired to do and therefore don't know when they are not doing it.

Don't sit in your office except when you really need to be there. Walk around, talk to people about what they're doing and how they feel about it. Know what's going on. And know everyone's name. Everyone's first name. Let them know that you notice when they do well. But don't hover. Let them do their job. Allow them to have control over the work for which they're responsible. People need to feel they have a degree of autonomy and that they are trusted. Only if the work is badly done do you need to intervene.

When you do criticize an employee, do so clearly, specifically, and decisively, but end the discussion on a positive note. Let him know that you have confidence in his ability to do the job well.

Gossip, rumor, jealousy, paranoia, backbiting, almost all these common office ills can be prevented by clear communication. If you are truly an accessible executive, rumor becomes unnecessary, because people can come to you directly. If the ground rules for promotions and raises are clear to everyone, then jealousy over one person's getting a raise and another person's not getting one can be largely put to rest. And if people know that you (assuming you're the boss in this scenario) are concerned about them, informed about their performance record, and determined to deal honestly with people, then the incentive for backbiting and *sotto voce* complaining will tend to disappear.

Get to know the workers, but don't involve yourself in the minutiae of their marital or social problems. The key, as always, is balance, letting people know you care about them without turning yourself into their psychiatrist or confessor.

Learn to get the gist, to make a quick read of a person's strengths and weaknesses; and later, do a meditation on that person to recheck your first hunch. Maybe this employee should be given different duties. Your intuition will tell you.

The office atmosphere always improves when workers feel that they're getting a fair shake and that their boss is practicing what he preaches. If, as head of the department, you let it be known you'll be in the office at nine, show up at nine. If you want your people to cut back on the long lunches, don't take three-hour lunches yourself.

If you happen to run the company, you get to make up the rules. But then follow them. Otherwise, you'll find yourself with a morale problem that can threaten the whole operation.

Managing people is a delicate and crucially important job. In perhaps no other facet of corporate life is intuition so essential to doing the job right. In developing that faculty, you are insuring, not only your own success, but the success atmosphere of the company as a whole.

15 Psyching Up Your Work Force

Creating a positive office environment is almost a prerequisite for business success; but as an inner executive, you want to go beyond conventional success, moving your company into the intuition-based business thinking of the next century. You want to give your whole work force the intuitive edge.

But you will probably have to start gradually. As we've mentioned, many people are uncomfortable with terms such as meditation and extrasensory perception, so don't use those words at first. Allow people their psychological comfort zones. Instead of "ESP," you might speak of "hunches." Instead of "meditation," say "relaxation." The techniques will work regardless of what you call them. The best scenario is to offer your workers three different seminars, emphasizing that their participation is entirely voluntary. The first is a "stress management seminar," the second a "group think" or what I call a "psychic suggestion box," and the third a guided "visualization session."

For each of these sessions, you should bring in an outside expert. Don't attempt to conduct them yourself, lest your presence be an intimidating influence and create reluctance in the very people you wish to inspire. You don't want them to think this is "one of the boss's crazy ideas." Whoever you bring in will have his or her own teaching style. In the present discussion, I am simply describing the approach I use when I go into corporations. It will not be exactly the same as someone else's approach.

THE STRESS MANAGEMENT SEMINAR

This program might run for a week or two, with a limited number of volunteers at each session. Perhaps it could be worked out so that each person gets to attend one class every few days for the duration of the training period. After that, he should be able to do the techniques by himself.

The optimum number of people is ten or twelve in each session. The program may be administered at the company—perhaps in the conference or exercise room—or it could be worked into a special stress-management weekend, during which the whole department is taken to a country retreat for a controlled series of bull sessions and training exercises.

If I were the trainer, I would first discuss the issues of tension and stress on the job and their effects on productivity and health. Then I would get right into the exercises. In my seminars I take a double approach: first, using the body to relax the mind, and then using the mind to relax the body.

A good way to start is to lead the group in a "tense and release" exercise of the kind outlined in Chapter One of this book. That's the one in which you clench your fists as hard as you can, to the count of eight, then relax your hands completely as you breathe out the words, "I let it go." You then tense and release each part of the body in turn, from your toes up to your face muscles, and with each relaxation you say, "I let it go."

A second way to use the body to relax the mind is to do the "deep breathing" exercise, also found in Chapter One. With this exercise, you breathe in slowly from the diaphragm, to the count of eight, then slowly breathe out. You do this three times, alternating these long deep breaths with normal breaths.

After letting everyone take a short break, I then move on to

160

exercises that use the mind to relax the body. These will be similar to the "making contact" exercise that concludes Chapter Two. The members of the seminar will be asked to close their eyes and visualize a bright screen, and then to begin counting down from ten to one, sinking deeper into their calm inner self with each count. I now lead them through the next part of the exercise, in which they imagine their bodies slowly filling with a warm white light, from their feet up to the top of their head.

They will then be invited to get acquainted with their inner self, to sense strongly its presence, and to feel the calmness at the center of their being. They should allow themselves a few minutes to get comfortable in that state, to feel at home there, since future exercises will involve entering into this consciousness level again. This is each person's private corner of the universe, with its own pathways, flowers, colors, aromas, and profound feelings of safety and love. Group members are encouraged to "flesh out" this subjective Eden in their own minds. The trainer will then bring the members of the group back "down to earth," counting slowly from five down to one. Many people find themselves feeling refreshed and stress-free, as if waking up from a wonderful dream.

THE PSYCHIC SUGGESTION BOX

If the first seminar helps workers conquer stress, this second session can help them use that relaxed state to access their intuition for the purpose of solving company problems. Again, a small number of people is optimum. Each should be supplied with a pad and pencil.

Before beginning, it is important to define one clear question that everyone will be seeking an answer to. It might be something like, How can the company increase its sales by 20 percent in the next year? Or, How can we significantly reduce the overhead? Or, What can be done to make the office operate more efficiently?

The next step is to do a meditation, again on the order of the "making contact" exercise from Chapter Two. When everyone has reached a state of relaxation, has felt himself filling with light, and has sensed the presence of his subconscious self, that's when the trainer poses the question of the day.

No one should say or write anything yet, because that would take them out of the meditative state. They should simply hold the question in their minds and allow images, thoughts, and hints to arise of their own volition. I might, however, introduce certain techniques at this point to help jog the intuitive faculties. If the participants are advertising people, and if the task is to come up with a new campaign, I might suggest that they visualize a TV set and "see" the new ad campaign on the screen. A group of car designers might be told to imagine a car hidden under a covering. Slowly, the covering is pulled away. What does the car look like?

After five or ten minutes in this quiet "waking trance" state, I slowly lead the seminar members back to everyday consciousness. That's when each person should jot down whatever he remembers, no matter how extraneous the images or thoughts may seem. There is no penalty for "stupid" ideas. No censorship, only sharing.

The "psychic suggestion box" idea might be implemented on two levels. One level might be for volunteers from the general population of the company, everyone from secretaries to supervisors. The other might be for an inner group of proven "idea people." It is to this second group that you might introduce the concepts of the inner child, and ESP, and the other terminology used in this book.

Those in the general group who come up with original or usable suggestions should be rewarded for their contributions; and if they continue coming up with good ideas, you might want to promote them to the inner group, with its more concentrated ESP activity. Psychic ability crosses all kinds of lines, educational as well as professional, and you may find that the most intuitive person in the company works in the mailroom. Always be ready to recognize and promote raw talent, wherever it may appear.

You might go even further in setting up a system of incentives, perhaps using the company newsletter to publicly congratulate the person with the "Suggestion of the Month"; or rewarding him or her with a special parking space; or offering free lunches in the cafeteria. And don't forget that person when raise or bonus time comes around. The inner child likes a game that has stakes and tangible rewards.

That child part of us also feels motivated when it is part of a team. Much of the boredom problem in offices stems from the fact that the workers don't feel that they are active agents in what's going on. No one, perhaps, has ever asked them if they have an idea. To have the boss actively soliciting their opinions and intuitions is likely to come as a refreshing shock; it changes the whole polarity of the employer-employee relationship.

After all, down in the trenches is where the problems are seen close up, and where solutions frequently present themselves. Yet in most companies the word seldom trickles up to the decision-making level. In one "psychic suggestion box" session, the group was asked to think of ways to cut back on expenditures. One worker piped up, "Why not sell some of the inventory we've been tripping over for the past ten months?" It turned out there was $1.3 million in inventory just sitting neatly in cartons on the floor. No one had paid attention to it.

THE VISUALIZATION SESSION

One of the most powerful ways to psyche up the work force is to teach them the basic techniques of creative visualization. Again, the groups should be kept quite small. It's best if the members are from the same department, so that they can visualize the same goals.

Suppose, for instance, you have a group from the sales department. I would start them off with a relaxation, and then talk to them about sales, explaining that thought creates money, and that the way you think about yourself and your clients determines the amount of money you will make. If you think of yourself as a person who brings in $10,000 worth of

163

sales per month, and the person in the adjoining office thinks of himself as a person who lands $100,000 in sales each month, guess which of you will be making the most sales.

To take a simple example, I recently went into a shoe store. It was a Saturday, and I happened to be wearing jeans and an old shirt. The saleswoman took one look at me and went into the back room and got herself a cup of coffee. The other salesperson, meanwhile, came right over to me full of enthusiasm and asked if he could help me. I ended up buying two pairs of shoes, and as he rang up the sale I could see that the woman was fuming, because she'd missed out. But he was the one who was prepared to sell. He saw a buyer; she saw a browser.

I emphasize in my seminars that people tend to buy when the person doing the selling is enthusiastic, knowledgeable, polite, and full of positive energy. It's really the energy of joy, because it comes from tapping into one's own life force.

The session would then go on to illustrate the techniques of creative visualization and the value of affirmations.

Frequently, at this point, I invite the salespeople to visualize a whole sales presentation, starting with the moment they open their eyes in the morning. I urge them to imagine themselves bouncing out of bed full of enthusiasm for the "game" of salesmanship that they'll be playing.

I then suggest that they start with a feeling of love for people. I tell them, "See yourself hugging your wife or husband and setting off with the attitude that you want to share your feelings of love with the people you're going to meet.

"Visualize the way you will be dressed, the snappy new attaché case you'll be carrying, the bounce in your step as you head to work.

"Visualize the person you will be making the sales pitch to and choose to view him, not as an adversary but as a trusted friend. See his look of pleasure as you enter his office (or boardroom or factory, etc.). See yourself making contact with his central child-self, the part of him that responds easily to someone who is both serious and filled with the spirit of play.

"Visualize the meeting, not as an attempt to sell him something, but as an offer to share something with him, an invitation for him to join you in a mutually beneficial game.

"See yourself full of confidence in your product, and as knowledgeable about his business as about your own. You will have digested all the relevant research about his business operation before this meeting takes place; and you will have meditated on what you learned, divining your client's needs and even his secret wishes. See yourself helping him to see what he *doesn't* want as well as what he does. Make it clear that your primary goal is not to sell him something, but to help him prosper in his business.

"Visualize yourself visualizing him as prosperous. Make that wish strong and real to yourself. Pray for his success.

"There is no sales approach more powerful than this, especially when combined with an honest excitement about your own product. Visualize yourself and your client warmly shaking hands and smiling. Know that you have not only made a sale, you have made a lifelong customer."

Often, I conclude the seminar by leading the group in a series of chanted affirmations. These might include the following:

Enthusiasm is the most contagious form of electricity.
I am selling a wonderful and exciting product.
This product is exactly what the customer needs for his own success.
I establish an easy rapport with the client's playful inner self.
I instantly psych into my client's business need.
It is a pleasure to be selling this product.
It is a privilege to help other people succeed.

16 : Hiring and Firing

If one were to pick the two most nerve-wracking jobs for an executive, they would probably be hiring and firing. That's true whether you're the manager of a candy store or the President of the United States. In fact, the nation begins to judge a new president on the basis of what people he brings into his cabinet and appoints to key posts. At the 1988 Democratic convention, Michael Dukakis got everyone to their feet cheering when he declared: "If you accept the privilege of public service, you had better understand the responsibilities of public service. If you violate that trust, you'll be fired; if you violate the law, you'll be prosecuted."

The better the job of hiring, of course, whether in the private or the public sector, the less frequent the need for firing. But determining the best person to hire for a given job can be extremely dicey. Résumés, as many personnel directors will admit, are largely fictional, even if all the facts they contain are true. They are, in effect, advertisements for the job candidate. They accentuate the positive, downplay the negative, and give *no* indication of how the person will behave in a crisis. They don't even tell you how he'll behave on a rainy Tuesday morning when his car has broken down.

So you have to rely on other indicators, such as appearance, personality, and the recommendations of former employers. But these are not very reliable guides, either. Some people interview well, are witty and relaxed, but lack the steadiness required for the job. Other people feel awkward being interviewed, but might be perfect once they're a part of the organization. That's why, if you are the one doing the hiring, you need to apply your ESP techniques to the hiring process. If the hiring is done by a personnel department, it will be necessary to teach those techniques to the head of that department, as well as to his or her senior staff. A revolutionary idea for most companies, true; but revolution, or at least evolution, in business thinking is what this book is about. Companies simply expend too many resources, waste too much time, and lose too much money training, supervising, and ultimately firing people who should never have been hired in the first place.

"Every time you add one key employee, make it the biggest, soundest decision of the year," advises Harvey Mackay in *Industry Week* magazine. Mackay is CEO of Mackay Envelope Corporation and a well-known author. "This keeps the probability the highest that he's going to be around. Business divorces, you know, are way higher than domestic divorces. You can't build a business with a revolving door." It's been my experience that if you have a good personnel team you'll almost always have a successful company. But if you have people in personnel who don't care, or who can't recognize talent unless it comes in wearing a three-piece suit and clutching a sheaf of credentials, your company is in danger. The best talent will be going out the revolving door and less competent people will be coming in.

PICKING THE BEST PEOPLE

Suppose you're trying to fill a key position in the production department. After sifting through hundreds of résumés and conducting a dozen interviews, you have narrowed the candidates to three men and two women. All seem equally qualified.

That's when you do a meditation on the problem. You close the door, sit comfortably in your straight-backed chair, and go into your private ritual for reaching the alpha state. This may involve doing a breathing exercise to relax, followed by the "countdown" exercise leading you step by step into the subconscious. Once you have established a solid feeling of contact with your inner self, you are ready to consider the candidates for the production job, meditating on them one by one. You don't dismiss any image or words that may occur to you; you don't deny any feeling. And when you come out of the meditation, you quickly scribble down all the impressions that you remember.

Look at them now. One of the male candidates brought to mind for some reason the image of a melting block of ice on the kitchen floor. Thinking about him, you realize you found him a little "cold" during the interview, a bit proud, and, somewhere under the surface, unhappy. The job happens to require a good deal of teamwork and the ability to explain production procedures to others. You realize that this man is not temperamentally suited to the task.

The other four still seem pretty equally matched, although you aren't sure why you visualized one of the women with a head cold. She hadn't had the sniffles when you interviewed her. You will do a follow-up meditation on these people later, but now you decide to go on to a second technique, the use of the pendulum. (See Chapter Thirteen for a more detailed discussion of pendulum techniques.)

Facing north, you place one applicant's photograph or résumé before you on the cleared desk and hold the pendulum above it. Ask your subconscious self about him or her. Is this the person for the job? If the pendulum begins moving from side to side, the answer is no. If it moves up and down the picture (like a nodding head), the answer is yes.

Let us say that two of the five candidates came up with a positive reading; the other three (including the man associated with the ice block and the woman with the sniffles) came up negative. You decide to go on to a third technique, that of dream imaging. (A quick review of Chapter Nine will tell you in more detail how that technique works.)

At bedtime, you hold in your mind the images of the five job candidates and ask your subconscious self for dream guidance in making a choice among them. You repeat the request three times, concentrating hard each time, then drink a couple of sips from the small glass of water by your bedside, close your eyes, and go to sleep.

Let's say you wake up with a welter of images and feelings. Quickly, you take another swallow of the water (triggering the subconscious recall), then pick up your pen and notebook and dash down everything you can remember. Much of it seems irrelevant, but you do recall the image of a woman you knew in college walking briskly down the street and smiling, her hair swinging and catching the sunlight. She pulled open the glass doors of a building and went inside. Thinking about it now, you realize it did not look like your company's building, but it somehow *felt* like it. And the old college acquaintance reminds you of one of the women candidates for the job. The brief dream sequence had a positive, happy feeling. You begin to think that maybe she is the person for the job.

Before making your decision, though, you decide to go through the three steps one more time. The results are congruent with the first round, and you feel confident to go ahead.

One last thing still bothers you, though. Why did the other woman (the one you didn't hire) appear in your imagery as having a head cold? You decide to make a couple of calls to people who knew her in her previous job. You discover she was frequently out sick, especially toward the end of her time there. Aha, susceptible to colds, then? It turns out there was more to it. Someone finally levels with you and tells you she had a drug problem, specifically cocaine. Half her salary was disappearing up her nose.

You thank your stars—and you especially thank your inner child—for the warning.

* * *

169

If substance abuse is a looming question in the hiring process, it's an even larger factor in the decision to fire a person. Increasing numbers of corporations are learning the art of tightrope walking between the right to individual privacy and the perceived need for drug testing in the workplace. There's no doubt that such testing will increase in the future, particularly for sensitive jobs; but many people with drug problems manage to pass those tests. That's why managers must be able to recognize the behavioral signs of addiction, and why they need to add intuitive techniques to their arsenal of managerial skills. Often, the subconscious picks up signals too subtle for the conscious mind to notice. The above example of the cocaine-addicted job candidate was presented as hypothetical, but it is based on an actual incident. If it weren't for subconscious signals, that woman might have been hired.

There are generally four stages in a manager's handling of an unsatisfactory employee:

1. Discerning the problem.
2. Defining the problem.
3. Confronting the problem.
4. Resolving the problem.

Some managers choose not to get to know their employees personally. The impersonal approach, they say, makes it less difficult to fire or transfer a worker if that becomes necessary. They cite the example of the judge who excuses himself from cases in which he has a personal interest, or the surgeon who will not operate on a family member. But the analogies sound more like rationalizations than like reasons. Being a manager is not about avoiding difficulty or emotional pain. The job has more in common with parenting than with either jurisprudence or incision-making.

"Give your people all the leeway they require, but keep yourself in a simple, hands-on position," suggests Leonard Lavin, Chairman/CEO of the Alberto-Culver Co., in an interview in *Industry Week*. He doesn't think much of executives "who manage by objective and sit back and wait for the reports to come in." I agree. I don't see how a manager can do his job without first-hand information about those who toil with him in

170

the same department. The hands-on manager knows his people well enough to detect behavioral changes, slumps in performance, or increased absenteeism. He can discern problems before they grow into tragedies.

If you are the manager, your next task, after locating the problem, is to define it as narrowly and precisely as possible. What aspect of the job is the employee neglecting or botching? Does he or she seem distracted on the job? Is there actual hostility? At whom is it directed?

Once you have carefully described the symptoms, you are ready to do a meditation on them. The logical mind, by itself, might have trouble knowing whether a worker's frequent sleepiness on the job is the result of boredom, too much night life, a newborn baby, a second job, or an addiction to Quaaludes.

The next step is to confront the individual about his problem, but to do so without being confrontational. The meeting might take place in your office or over a quiet lunch; it doesn't matter, as long as the underlying tone is one of respect. After all, he was brought into the company because of his positive qualities. Presumably he still has those qualities. Explain exactly what you have observed of his behavior, and over what period of time, and ask if there are any problems he would like to talk over with you.

The whole thing may come out at this time. A woman who's been noticeably depressed for the past two months may explain that she recently had a baby and hasn't been able to shake off the postpartum blues. These things are understandable and, more to the point, they're temporary. As a manager, you can help your workers over such rough spots, perhaps giving them vacation time or getting them to a counselor.

A worker with a drug or alcohol problem is less likely to confess that fact to you. With such a person, you need to look at chronic behavior, mood swings, and changes in long-term relationships with coworkers. You may need to do further meditation sessions on his situation to test your hunches. If you care enough about your employee and consider him important to the company, you may need to contact his spouse or others who know him well.

Certainly you don't want to go on making excuses for this person, no matter how important he is to the company. That would make you an "enabler," as Alcoholics Anonymous puts it, and your actions would cause resentment among other workers who are not similarly treated.

The time must come when you have another meeting with this person, confront him about the addiction, and make it clear that he must clean up his act immediately. That means counseling, or a clinic, or whatever it takes. Place a time limit on it. Let your words be calm and empathetic and absolutely straightforward. He must get clean or get out.

The important thing in all these cases is to maintain effective communication. If a soft-hearted manager speaks vaguely about improvement, an alcoholic will see a loophole and not confront his problem. The point is not to be soft or hard on the workers, but to be always clear. "Give your full professional opinion as to what the problem is, what the solution might be, and don't pull your punches," urges Vaughn Beals, Jr., Chairman and CEO of Harley-Davidson, Inc., in a recent interview. The best managers have an element of impersonality in their business dealings. They achieve this, not by holding themselves apart from people, but by putting truth first.

One basic truth is that we create our own reality. A person who has become an unsatisfactory employee has created that situation; and on some level, he has done so because he wanted to. People sabotage themselves. In a sense, they fire themselves.

If it does become necessary to fire a worker, it may be helpful to do a visualization beforehand, to smooth the psychic path. It is wise to do this exercise a day or so ahead of time. Put yourself into a relaxed state and visualize the employee coming into your office. See yourself as calm, knowledgeable, and strong. You feel no anger at all, only positive feelings about this person's potential. You want him to fulfill that potential and hope that in his next job he'll be able to do so. You visualize the two of you rising and shaking hands. He leaves with his dignity intact.

This sort of visualization sets up a blueprint on inner planes and increases the likelihood that the meeting will go smoothly. But of course the exercise does not guarantee what his reaction will be. He may become angry, sullen, flippant, depressed. Your calm, positive approach will help him avoid such emotions, but ultimately how he reacts is up to him. You, at least, will have kept a steady center and greatly lessened the possibility of any long-term bitterness. Negative energy, if you allowed it into your heart, would be harmful to him, to you, and to your company.

These are volatile days for business. Corporate raiding, downsizing, financial reorganization, the zigzagging dollar, and global competition have transformed the once staid and stuffy corporate world into something like a gladiatorial contest in which it's hard to tell the Christians from the lions. It is a world in which Eastern Airlines can suddenly announce it is dropping 4,000 employees from its rolls (as it did in mid-1988), a world in which plant closings turn company towns into ghost towns. No one's job is completely secure.

It's a good idea, then, to give a thought to your own career and to what you might do if suddenly you had to find a new job. There is no doubt that many laid-off executives suffer economic hardships and a badly shaken self-image before they regain their footing in the business world. I don't want to minimize that. But there is also, on one level, something refreshing about starting over. The inner child perks up, gets interested, starts sending up intuitions and ideas you never thought you had.

If you're one of thousands of people laid off because of unexpected effects of the Japanese yen or some other distant cause, the loss of your job may feel like the loss of a ship in a typhoon. Nothing personal, lots of company, and nobody really to blame.

If, on the other hand, it is just you being fired, there's a considerably greater threat to your sense of self-worth. You have been rejected, found wanting. The temptation is either to blame the company for being unjust, cruel, and unappreciative or to blame yourself for your apparent shortcomings. As tempting as such options are, the inner executive will resist them, choosing to replace blame with responsibility. Stanley Pace, the

GERALD JACKSON

Chairman and CEO of General Dynamics Corporation, was not speaking of employment termination when he said, in a recent interview, that "to be successful in management, you must not only be willing but *eager* to accept responsibility. That means responsibility for success or failure." But his words apply more than ever to the person who has lost his job. Affixing blame is negative; taking responsibility is positive.

Before refurbishing your résumé or buying a copy of *What Color is Your Parachute?*, it would be a good idea to meditate on what signals you had been giving off and what was really behind your firing. Total honesty is the key here. While in the meditative state, you are in your private confessional speaking through the grill to your secret self—the one person who truly understands you.

Did you in some way make your firing inevitable? Did you unconsciously wish it to happen? Was the child part of you happy in that job or was it stifled? What does your inner child really want to do? You may think that you enjoyed your prestigious job in management, but maybe your child part was having more fun when you were back in sales. There was more of a creative challenge, more wind in your hair.

Most people find themselves stuck in jobs that are spiritually too small for them. They feel ready to graduate but are kept back, repeating the same grade, reading the same annual reports, year after year. So maybe the child sabotaged you—made you late, make you less deferential than some would like, gave you a temper.

Your firing, then, might be the culmination of an inner rebellion. It may be the best thing that you ever caused to happen. You've handed yourself the gift of a second chance; now take the opportunity and run with it!

17 Moving Up in the Company

We all need to feel that our lives are going somewhere, preferably forward, although "forward" signifies different things to different people—things as diverse as finding a love relationship, writing a novel, losing weight, designing a microchip, having a child, doing volunteer work for persons with AIDS. It can also mean moving up in the company. To know that there is no chance of advancement in a company would be demoralizing for most people. In such a situation, they may lose their motivation, become listless, resentful of management. There are businesses where the hierarchy is pre-established and significant advancement is not possible. And there are other places where a person who does one particular job well is kept in that slot indefinitely. (That happened to me some years back; finally I quit.) You want to use your intuition to psych out the advancement opportunities in your company. Will you be able to move ahead or not?

Not long ago, I counseled a man in radio sales who was working under a particularly oppressive sales manager. Not only was promotion unlikely, but the working atmosphere was unpleasant. My intuition about the situation was that the sales manager would soon be fired and that things would soon improve. As it happened, the manager did get fired a month or two later and was replaced by a bright, personable, and innovative person who doubled the station's sales and substantially increased the salespeople's salaries.

Your intuitions can tell you when it's worthwhile to wait out a situation and when you are better off changing divisions or even companies. But in order to make such decisions, you must know where it is you want to go. The wrong promotion can be as bad as no promotion at all. Be specific about your ambitions. Would you be happier managing a large department (and enjoying the more important title and heftier paycheck), or is your personality better suited to working by yourself or with a small team on specific projects?

Exercise: Visualizing Your Life Backward

People with fuzzy goals tend to manifest fuzzy results. They may find themselves, after years in a company, in a job slot they happened into in the course of routine promotions. If you want to choose your future, take some time to visualize it. The following meditation will help.

Find a private place where you will not be disturbed. Completely relax, doing a "tense-and-release" or a deep breathing exercise. Then go on to a countdown exercise to get yourself into a receptive, meditative state. When you are totally calm, inwardly quiet, and firmly grounded, visualize yourself decades in the future, at your retirement dinner.

What age are you? fifty-five? sixty-five? More? Set your own retirement age. How do you look? Are you in good health?

What about the people around you at the table? Do you recognize any of them from among your present colleagues? Is there a certain informality or irreverence to the proceedings, or is this a sumptuous formal event? When they stand up to speak, how do your colleagues describe your accomplishments?

What is your exact position in the company? Executive vice president? Chairman of the board? Or the best darn copywriter the advertising department ever had?

What will you have done for the company by that time? Will it look very different from the way it looks today? Do you see yourself as nationally known, your face on the cover of

Business Week or *Inc.* or *Forbes?* Or is your business fulfill-
ment of a more private sort? Whatever your ultimate goal,
visualize it clearly and in detail. Hold that image.

Then back up, mentally, to where you are today: your
position, your pay level, your immediate prospects. As you
contemplate the distance between your present job and your
ultimate goal, can you imagine a path that will lead you to that
goal, or does your subconscious send up the message: "You
can't get there from here"?

If you really can't get there, you are telling yourself to leave
the company and find one with more rapid escalators—or to
start a company yourself.

If you think you can reach your professional goals in your
present company, visualize as specifically as you can the steps
you will need to take, starting with the *next* step.

This exercise, as you can tell, is no longer pure ESP. You
are in an inwardly quiet, meditative state, in touch with your
psychic self, but you are also figuring. Poets and musicians do
this all the time when they are composing. They "test their
rhythms on their wrist," making sure that the structures they
are building always correspond to the basic pulse-beat of identity. They are looking for the lines that "feel right."

Take this process as far as you can, creating concrete
images in your mind concerning the next three or four career
steps you need to take. But don't attempt to do it all at once.
Repeat this exercise at regular intervals, seeing a little further
along the way each time.

In the intervals between your "backward visualization"
sessions, take some small positive steps to make the goal real
and to precipitate the mental image into the physical world.
The clearer the mental image, the easier it is to make it manifest. What you do depends on your personality. I've recom-
mended to some clients that they photocopy last year's W2
form and add a zero to the gross income. Allow yourself to see,
in other words, an income that is ten times what you are now
making.

Others have found it helpful to make up business cards
with their dream title under their name. If the goal is to become

chief sales representative, then have that printed. If it is to be executive vice president, then print that. It's a little psychic reinforcement to remind you of where you are headed. Prudence would suggest, however, that you don't hand these cards out just yet.

Executives often speed their rise through the ranks by finding a mentor who recognizes their potential and looks out for their interests. Such an arrangement can be wonderfully helpful, provided there is no *quid pro quo*. But before pursuing this approach, it is well to do a meditation, and perhaps to ask the subconscious for dream guidance as well. You don't want to go wrong on this one.

Don't pick a mentor who is going to leave the company, unless he or she is going to take you along to the new company. When former CBS News President William Small was hired to be the news president at NBC, he brought so many people over with him that there was a hemorrhage of talent at CBS. Ultimately, though, he proved a less useful mentor than he seemed at first. The CBS invaders were resented at NBC, and Small's abrasive personality failed to endear him to NBC's news veterans. Before long he was out, and so were many of the CBS-ers he had sponsored.

Don't pick a mentor whose own career is stalled. Some vice presidents will never be executive vice presidents. They've risen as far as they are going to. If *they* are being passed over, you can figure that the people they sponsor will be passed over, too.

Don't psych into the company renegade, the maverick with the great ideas and the lousy manners. He's probably there on sufferance, because of the particular skills he has. His personnel recommendations are unlikely to be heeded. He's a guy to attach yourself to only if you want to leave with him and start a new company. But then you've got to deal with his personality on a permanent basis. Meditate well before getting into a situation like that.

An acquaintance of mine in the cosmetics industry hitched his career to a company star, a very talented woman. Unfortunately, her own career goal was to make enough money to retire by the time she was fifty. This she proceeded to do, leaving her protégé high and dry. Know your mentor's own career intentions.

Such considerations are worth careful contemplation and repeated ESP exercises if you are planning to get somewhere in the company. It is not a question of manipulation. Mentors know they are mentors; they know they are being useful. Ideally, they are helping you because they want the best people in top management. And there is, of course, a certain amount of politics involved: they prove their power by having protégés, and they look good if you make good. As Merle Banta, Chairman/CEO of AM International, Inc., put it recently in *Industry Week,* "Some people are fearful of hiring [or helping along] good people below them. That's a terrible mistake—the better people you have, the better *you're* going to do."

That's the kind of thinking that makes for successful companies. Companies also benefit when people help along colleagues who are on their same level. This is not a mentor relationship, but a networking among equals. It's true that in many places there is an implicit competition for promotions, but that's an organizational model that needs to be changed. Sometimes defended as the survival of the fittest, the old dog-eat-dog mentality results in an erosion of the necessary infrastructure of cooperation. There's nothing to be gained by viewing your colleague as a threat. Share some information you have which your coworker might need. Praise his or her work to your boss. It feels good. It makes your colleague feel good. In the long run, it makes you *look* good.

We all know, however, of instances of favoritism. Let's say you're in there doing a great job, and the boss's nephew gets out of college and is handed the job you were being considered for. Such things happen, and if it happens to you, you need your keenest intuitions to know how to proceed. You may sense that it's best to wait it out, that the new golden boy is inept and will self-destruct before the year is out. Or you may come up with an intuition about how to advance by some other avenue, possibly in another department. Or you may realize that this boulder is going to sit in your path for the next twenty years and

179

that you'd be better off going across the street and working for the competition.

I advise my business clients to be the best at what they do and to make this the primary goal, because that will always proclaim their value to the company. But I also advise them to be political, keep their noses to the wind, and their antennae waving. It may not be enough anymore to be a great research scientist at Dupont and yet be totally unaware of who is being promoted, what direction the company is moving in, and whether Dupont is plotting a takeover of Gulf + Western.

And whatever you do, never, never make an enemy of your secretary. The people you depend on to do things for you can make you look like a genius or an idiot. If you are disliked by these people, you may find that the crucial information you need for a meeting is placed on your desk an hour after the meeting is over. The company car might be in the shop the day you need it. The communications center may suddenly have problems with the Fax machine. Your secretary may call in with the flu the very day your all-important twenty-page report must be typed.

If, on the other hand, you have made staunch allies of your support staff, the secretary will come in to work in a snowstorm, flu or no flu, to get your report done. No one moves up in a company without the help of others. Be a hero to those others, go to bat for them, listen to their problems, and they will make you a hero to your superiors. "So often, people don't respect their superiors and they run them down to their people," commented Richard Ringoen, chairman/CEO of the Ball Corporation, in a recent interview. "That is terribly detrimental. In order for an organization to work, each person in it has to respect and try to help everybody else. . . . If everybody's trying to get his or her boss promoted, that organization's really working."

Meanwhile, in your efforts to get yourself promoted, find a way to showcase your abilities. I'm not saying you should be a braggart or pretend to virtues you don't possess; but when you come up with an idea that saves the company significant money, or speeds the traffic, or improves the firm's image in the community, find a way to make that fact known to the right people. If you have a mentor, or a positive and mutually helpful relationship with your colleagues, perhaps they will blow your horn for you.

In companies where jealousy, brownnosing, and backstabbing are intramural sports, such mutual support among workers may be difficult to imagine. That's because most businesspeople still assume that there is only so much to go around and that for one person to win another person must lose. In Earth's ecosystem, there is no lack, except that created by mankind. There is enough food to feed the world, if governments would cooperate. And there is enough room in a well-run company for all workers to rise to the level of their potential.

But "lack" is a seductive belief; it scratches all our basest itches. You can feel it yourself the next time you catch a glimpse of a colleague's paycheck and realize that she is making more money than you are. Your mind immediately scrambles to figure out what she is doing that you are not. You may feel deprived, even though, five minutes before, you might have been feeling pretty good about your own salary. If she has more, does that mean you have less?

As an inner-executive-in-training, you no doubt already realize the need to break out of this destructive belief system and to help others do the same. And you can teach them by the way you conduct yourself in the company. They will see that while some people are clawing and scratching their way up the corporate ladder—and nursing ulcers along the way—you rise to the top like cream. And the futility of blindsiding and downgrading one's coworkers will become obvious to all when you are seen moving up through the ranks by a system of goal-setting, creative visualization, intuition, and generosity.

Don't expect this to happen overnight. You may be viewed with some suspicion the first time you share information with a coworker when keeping it to yourself would have given you an advantage. But when it becomes clear that that's the way you operate, watch relief break out all over. And watch the energy you send out come back to you in the form of loyalty from subordinates, collegiality from those on your level, and the surprised admiration of those above you in the organization. Business, after all, is a game, one to be played hard, but by the rule book. The rules are simple: Don't hurt anyone; don't sell your soul.

Your success is proof that you don't have to.

18 Business Trips

Travel refreshes the senses and challenges the inner child, which is why I find pleasure trips a spur to my intuitive faculties. Business trips, however, used to be a different story. They were a major source of anxiety—first, facing the trains, planes, and automobiles that would take me to my destination, then sleeping in an unfamiliar hotel room, and finally braving the scary business meeting the next day. It was an experience in which, in Dr. Johnson's phrase, there was "more to be endured than to be enjoyed."

Well, I am still not enamored of business trips, but I've learned some tricks to turn Dr. Johnson's words around. There's now more to enjoy, less to endure.

The secret, I've found, is to let yourself be guided each step of the way by your intuition. The next time a business trip is proposed, I suggest doing a meditation in which you ask your intuitive child-self if the trip is really necessary, if it could be dangerous, if this is a good time of year to go, how long you should plan on being away, and which days are the best for traveling.

Some of the answers you get may have as much to do with common sense as with intuition. If you're an author or book agent, you probably wouldn't go to New York in May to knock on the doors of publishers, because they'll be away at the spring convention of the American Booksellers Association. But sometimes the hunches you get about travel go beyond common to uncommon, even uncanny, sense. A few years ago, I was planning a business trip to Florida, but when I did a meditation on it I came up with images of snow and slippery conditions. Snow in Ft. Lauderdale? I called the National Weather Service and learned that, yes, it was going to be colder than normal, but no snow was expected. Nevertheless, I cancelled the trip—and it *did* snow in Ft. Lauderdale that week.

So consult yourself, using the techniques in this book. And then take your own advice. I would also consult *The Old Farmer's Almanac* to find out the time of the new moon. As I mentioned in Chapter Twelve, the earth's energy is very positive during the first few days of the new moon. Plants tend to grow; plans tend to succeed.

Once you've determined the optimum time for your trip, read up on the area and do further meditations on the best hotel to book. The reason for invoking your intuitive powers in this case concerns more than just the comfort or convenience of the hotel. It can also relate to business syncronicities, such as whether you'll meet an important new business contact by staying at one place rather than at another. I often use the pendulum for this part of the planning. I hold it over a drawing of an encircled cross and ask about each hotel in turn.

Finally, a day or two before leaving, do a "safety visualization," to clear away psychic obstacles and to establish an impulse or inner pattern for a smooth trip. Get into a relaxed state, establish a strong feeling of centeredness, then visualize yourself boarding the airplane. Envision everyone in a good mood, see yourself in the seat you prefer, see the plane taking off smoothly, having a safe and easy flight, and landing perfectly. Visualize your luggage coming out of the carousel, see yourself meeting your contact, and the two of you smiling and shaking hands, hitting it off right away.

Remember, visualizing is not simply wishing; it is preparing yourself on inner planes so that your outer plane will take off and land without problems. I cannot explain "scientifically" why it should work. I only know that if you put out positive, specifically directed energy, you get positive results back.

If you're going to a part of the world where there's been political unrest or anti-American demonstrations, you need to pay particular attention to your intuition. If you have nightmares involving travel, I'd suggest trusting your gut feeling and calling off the trip, if at all possible. We've all heard of cases where people had warning dreams and at the last moment, against all "reason," cancelled their passage on the *Titanic,* the *Andrea Doria,* the *Achille Lauro.* If you receive such a warning, conduct your business by phone. Send the contract by Federal Express. Or if you absolutely must go, try to delay the trip by a few days, until your intuitions about it become more positive. Of course, delaying may not be a realistic option, given your responsibilities to your company. Later in this chapter we discuss ways to maximize the safety and success of any trip— even one which your subconscious advises you against.

When you travel, be sure to remember that business is still going on at home. That means careful delegation of responsibilities to ensure that all goes well in your absence. Many CEOs or COOs are poor delegators. They don't trust the judgment, or even the loyalty, of subordinates. In some companies this is a legitimate fear; usurpers try to undermine or supplant the absent executive. In one particularly volatile media company, a joke was making the rounds for a while: An executive buzzes his secretary and barks: "Miss Fitch, if my boss calls, be sure to get his name." Such companies are in serious trouble. You must have people, or at least someone, that you can really trust to mind the store, or your trip will be a nightmare of anxiety.

Mary Wells Lawrence, one of the founders of the powerhouse ad agency, Wells, Rich, Greene, has learned the lesson of delegating. As she told *Advertising Age* recently, "I felt very strongly that if other people were going to come up, I would have to get my ego down in size and swallow it and pull back and let other people shine. . . . It's hard to do because people don't want to let you do it." She calls in regularly, however, even from the south of France. Anyone making a trip away from the corporate base should do the same. And of course leave phone numbers where you can be reached at any time.

It hardly needs to be said that you also need to call home and talk to the people you care most about, keeping your psychic links strong. High-pressure business trips tend to be disorienting and upsetting to the subconscious; touching base with loved ones can relieve that stress, helping you to meditate more effectively and to keep your concentration on the business at hand. I even call home sometimes and talk to my dog. A friend puts her on the speakerphone and I reassure her with the sound of my voice (and she reassures me with her barks). My father used to call home every night when he was on business trips. He'd talk with my mother and then with each one of us, asking about our homework, making sure we all felt connected.

To counteract the disruptive aspects of travel, try to keep as many constants in your life as possible. For example, continue as before doing your ESP exercises. In fact, otherwise wasted hours at airports or on buses are a perfect time to center yourself and sharpen your intuitive skills. Can you psych out what sort of person will be sitting next to you on the plane? What color will he or she be wearing? What will be the first message waiting for you at the hotel? What will the view be from your window?

And be sure to keep up your rituals. If you normally have a full Texas breakfast, don't rush out in the morning fueled only with a cup of black coffee. If you're on a diet, don't go off it. If you usually work out in a gym, arrange to do the same in the city you're in. If you've gotten in the habit of meditating twice a day, don't let that habit slip. (In fact, it's more important now than ever.)

People often throw their whole psychology, as well as their physiology, out of whack when they go on trips. They start eating things they don't normally eat and doing things they don't normally do. They confuse the subconscious and thus make it extremely difficult to access their intuition.

This is a particular danger during those strange events known as conventions. It's often thought that the usual rules don't apply and that the appropriate conventional behavior is unconventional behavior. Don't believe it. A person who is centered, in touch with his inner self at all times, will behave consistently and with a natural sense of dignity, no matter what the circumstances. Heavy drinking, rowdiness, and promiscuity are not big temptations for someone who is at ease with himself. Colleagues who are officious and ultraproper in the home office but wild men or women at conventions are demonstrating that they are uncentered, inconsistent, and in a sense inauthentic. If they were truly themselves in their daily work lives, they would not need to compensate with wild behavior swings.

Any senior executive who is present at such a convention would be inclined to rule out certain people for important promotions down the road. He'd realize they couldn't be trusted to represent the company in a high position. Conventions, then, can provide opportunities for "psychic spying," for seeing sides of people usually kept hidden. Even if the chief operating officer is not present, word has a way of getting back.

Travel, then, can hold dangers of quite a different sort than getting your luggage mixed up at the airport. To minimize such dangers and maximize your periods of pleasure, I would offer two additional bits of advice: First, don't try to economize; and, second, find out everything you can about the place you're going to.

DON'T ECONOMIZE

Schedule in an extra day, preferably after the business meetings are concluded, and use it for going to the beach, playing golf, doing something to reward the inner child for making the trip in the first place. If the playful part of you has something to look forward to, you'll feel psyched up and energized throughout the trip.

You also don't want to arrive the day of the important meeting. If the meeting's on Monday, try to get into town

Sunday afternoon, to acclimate yourself and get rested. You need to be at the top of your game Monday morning.

For the same reason, don't skimp on the hotel. Depressing accommodations can take the spring right out of your step, and a lumpy mattress can spoil your sleep. Remember, you haven't come all this way to save money, but to make money; and the way to make money is to be overflowing with positive energy.

If you have correspondence to take care of or contracts to redraft, you might do well to have your secretary travel with you and take charge of the details so that you can concentrate on the main business. The expense of the extra ticket and the extra room may be more than offset by lucrative deals you are able to conclude.

PSYCH OUT THE LOCALE

If you're going to a city you've never been to before, read up about the place, what the city is most proud of, how the hometown ball club is doing, what the municipal government is like. Then do a meditation on this information, to form a clear feeling about the town. Psyching out the locale can help you psych into the people you'll be dealing with at your business meetings. If you're from up north, your franchise talks in Atlanta will go better if you have a sense of how Southerners think and what issues are important to them.

If you're an Atlantan who's coming to New York for the first time, it's a good idea to know some of the unspoken rules of New York life (e.g., don't expect taxi drivers to speak English; don't wear expensive necklaces in the subway; don't take the subway). Many people from gentler climes are frightened when they come to rough-and-tumble megalopolises like New York or Chicago. One woman I know came to New York from Kansas; she walked around with her hands in fists, ready to slug the first mugger to dart out from a dark alley.

But fearfulness is as counterproductive as country gullibility. We attract what we project; we draw to us what we fear. And those who come to New York, Detroit, or Chicago expecting an unpleasant experience will assuredly have an unpleasant experience. That's why creative visualization, supported by some accurate information about the place, can make a tremendous difference. Before you arrive in the big city, walk yourself mentally through your whole stay there—including the wonderful French restaurant you intend to try and the play you plan to see. Create a realistically optimistic scenario and blueprint it in your subconscious. Events will naturally alter that scenario somewhat, but perhaps not very much. A positive, upbeat attitude and an openness to people will help make your trip a success, even a pleasure. Such an attitude creates a psychic shield against the negativity that all major cities contain to a greater or lesser extent.

Come well-briefed and well-prepared, with plenty of advance work. Bring extra shirts, extra ties, extra pantyhose, just in case, on the morning of the big meeting, you happen to spill your breakfast tomato juice or get a run in your stockings.

THE FORCE FIELD

Behind the visible, physical world lies a world of energy, comprised of the unseen but powerful forces of love, hatred, joy, good, evil. These unseen human energies impress themselves upon the environment, which is why one house feels good to a prospective buyer, even if it doesn't *look* particularly good, and another house feels somehow unfriendly. I felt the most negative energy of my life when I visited the Tower of London, where horrible crimes had once been committed and many people had died. I couldn't get out of there fast enough.

The reason for mentioning this is that you don't know who has slept in your hotel room before you. Probably some bored Willie Loman with his sample case, but possibly it was a suicide preparing to blow his brains out. If you have any queasy feeling about the psychic atmosphere of your room, ask to be switched to a different room. If that isn't possible, try the following procedure for psychically "airing out" the room.

189

First record the italicized instructions on your tape recorder, then play them back and let your own voice lead you through the exercise.

Exercise: Clearing Out Negative Energy

Find a comfortable seat in the room. Close your eyes and take several slow deep breaths to relax yourself; then do a countdown from ten to one, sinking deeper into the meditative state. Feel yourself "touching bottom" inside yourself, in contact with your essential identity. Then imagine the room becoming suffused with a white pure light. Visualize the light pushing away all the negative thoughts, leftover anger, stale emotions that may have been in the room before.

Feel your own body filling with this same white energy, becoming positively charged so that negative thoughts cannot adhere to you or find a place in your consciousness. Hold that image of pure, positive, white energy, and feel the whole room glowing with it.

Then, with your eyes still closed, gradually allow yourself to become aware of the texture of the chair you're sitting on, the sounds from outside the window. Count slowly from five to one, as you return to your normal consciousness.

Open your eyes.

PREPARING FOR THE MEETING

Another hotel activity very much worth doing the night before the business meeting is taking yourself through a creative visualization of that meeting, starting with a vision of yourself approaching the office building and ending with an image of the handshakes and smiles at the meeting's conclusion. Above all, see yourself getting what you came all this way to get. (See Chapter Seven for visualization techniques.)

When the moment for the meeting actually comes and you are about to go in, you may want to do a quick relaxation to dissipate your nervousness. Stand still, take a deep easy breath and as you exhale, whisper, "I let it go." Then take a normal breath. Repeat this procedure two more times, each time saying as you exhale, "I let it go."

Decide in your heart that you are going in to meet with friends—even if you've never met any of them before. To do so changes the polarity of the meeting. In his classic treatise, *Ich und Du,* philosopher Martin Buber spoke of the empathetic "I–Thou" relationship between people, as opposed to the depersonalized "I–It" relationship. In *The Power of Myth,* philosopher and mythologist Joseph Campbell elaborated on this distinction: "You can address anything as a Thou, and you can feel the change in your psychology as you do it. The ego that sees a Thou is not the same ego that sees an It. And when you go to war with a people, the problem for newspapers is to turn those people into Its, so that they're not Thous."

I'm not suggesting that you attempt to turn the business meeting into a mystical communion. Play hardball, if that's the game everybody's come out for; but play it with fully dimensional people, not with "the enemy." Make eye contact, find the potential friend within the adversary, the kid inside the three-piece suit. See the contest as a wonderful sporting event, and convey your sense of enjoyment to those present. It is amazing what such an approach can do to the atmosphere of even the toughest negotiations.

If you can do this, you'll return home, not just with a deal, but with a long-term business relationship that will bring you profits for years to come.

19 Sexual Politics in the Office

A man went into the hospital to have a sex-change operation. Afterwards, a friend visited him and asked, "What was the most painful part of the procedure? Was it the radical surgery?"

"No," moaned the patient.

"Was it when the anesthetic wore off?"

"No."

"Then what was it?"

"It was having my salary cut in half."

It's no joke. Women are entering the workplace in about the same numbers as men, but they're earning less in the same jobs. Often, they can't even get the same jobs. One male personnel manager, faced with a need to increase the secretarial staff, said in my hearing, "We'd better hire a few more girls." The sexism was quite unconscious, I'm convinced. He just assumed that secretaries would be female, and a certain kind of female—not "ladies," not "women," but "girls." The term is suggestive of class rather than age. In fact, if one of the secretaries hired happened to be a 55-year-old grandmother, the manager would no doubt refer to her as a "girl" along with the others.

The corporate world has always been a preserve of patriarchy, because until fairly recently the only high executives were men. Since that is no longer the case, attitudes are starting to change, but the changes have been slow. Men and women have always viewed one another with a touch of wariness, mixed with equal parts of attraction, condescension and superstition. The opposite sex is inherently peculiar. In the business world, the opposite sex is also threatening. Men are threatened, for instance, by recent successful court challenges to the all-male club, where a man could count on being able to put up his feet, light up a fine Havana, and chat with his business chums. The idea of women being admitted to such male sanctuaries seems almost sacrilegious to some.

The result of this attitude is that, for all the women now working in corporations, only a tiny percentage have made it to the top of their organizations. Most are concentrated in the lower paying, service jobs, and the rest are stuck somewhere in middle management, with little prospect of advancement.

The fact is, most *men* are also stuck somewhere in mid-corporation, and very few have ever been invited to join a club. The great majority of working men have more in common with working women than either camp realizes. But at least a man is allowed the myth of unlimited advancement. He may be just another white shirt at the water cooler, but he can dream of one day being a Donald Trump or a Lee Iacocca.

"You can't be a Lee Iacocca," women are taught early in their careers; "you can only marry a Lee Iacocca."

If they can't or won't do that, many women face subtle forms of discrimination in the workplace. Some become embittered by their experiences; others become resigned. Still others are so determined to beat the guys at their own game that they strive to be better than anyone else. That can be a healthy reaction, but too often it is really an overcompensation for a perceived handicap—the handicap of having been born female—and it can lead to stress, depression, and, for some, ultimately burn out.

Another side effect of stress is a short-circuiting of the intuition. It is ironic that women, who are always accused of (or

193

credited with) possessing "female intuition," may actually suppress that faculty in the workplace, where they may need it most.

Intuition is no more a female faculty than logic is a male faculty. Both are *human* faculties. Nor are they necessarily in opposition. Having said that, I must add that I do find women generally more intuitive than men. I'm not sure why this should be so. It may have something to do with our outmoded but still prevalent assumptions about raising children. Girls always used to be brought up to listen, to be sensitive, a bit whimsical, emotional. Boys were brought up to suppress or at least to suspect those qualities. While the boys were cudgeling their brains with physics and cudgeling their schoolmates on the playing field, girls were learning the impractical arts of poetry and music (both rich stimulants to the intuitive side of the psyche).

Such crude educational dichotomies have been on the way out for some time, but they're not gone yet; and they continue to affect unspoken attitudes about sex roles. A parent may say, and believe, "In our free society, my son can grow up to be President of the United States"; but that parent is less likely to say the same of his daughter. We have to get to the point in our thinking where we say, "My *child* can grow up to be president." We must raise our daughters, not to be secretaries, but to be Secretary of State.

And still be intuitive. For officeholders of the twenty-first century, a mastery of intuition will be as important as statecraft, an understanding of history, and a talent for rolling a pork barrel through Congress.

Even if a woman does not enter politics, she has automatically entered *office* politics as soon as she takes a job. If she is like most women, she will find herself undervalued, underpaid, and overworked. She may contribute to the problem by undervaluing herself. There is, after all, a strong tendency to view ourselves as we are viewed by others. Men do it too, of course. And in the vast gray area of middle management there are probably as many men who feel undervalued as there are women. That's one reason they may resent the rare woman who breaks out of their ranks and rises to vice president. They feel, "That should have been me," or, "She must have slept her way up," or, "Why don't women stay at home where they belong?"

They should be celebrating her rise in the company, not resenting it. It means the power structure is opening up just a bit more, and that can only help everyone.

If, as a woman, you find yourself more competent and better informed than some of the men you work with (or for), and yet defer to them constantly, you have some work to do on yourself. You may be suffering from the success/guilt syndrome—the sense that you are somehow not worthy of getting to the top. Subconsciously, you may be saying, "If no one else will stop me, I'll stop myself—by screwing up, by breaking down, by letting some male colleague take the credit or land the account."

Here is where affirmations can be valuable for a woman. (Review the discussion of affirmations in Chapter Six.) When you wake up in the morning, or whenever you think of it during the day, put yourself into a calm, relaxed state and say to yourself:

I am a powerful human being.
As a woman, I have an intuitive edge.
Being a woman is a tremendous asset.
I perform a valuable and essential service to the company.
My colleagues at work are my allies.
I command respect and admiration.
I am an excellent worker and am achieving great things.
I have a wonderful mission to fulfill.

Say these (or other more personally specific) affirmations over and over, whenever you think of them. Type them out and keep them where you can see them during the day.

Undervaluing yourself is the flip side of another common problem: overworking yourself. Many women work insanely long hours in order to catch up with the male executives, or to prove that they are not frail, ineffectual creatures. Unfortunately, overwork tends to generate stress, which is the great negator of intuition. If you find yourself in this predicament, review the two stress-reduction exercises at the end of Chapter One, and the color exercises in Chapter Eleven. They can help you in the short term, whenever you need a "stress fix." But you also need to find a long-term solution to the problem. Put yourself into a calm state of mind, then look dispassionately at the male/female dynamic at your office.

Is your office one of those in which terms like "intuition" or "ESP" would be treated with derision? If so, you are working among reactionaries and might do better to switch to a more open-minded work environment. But while you're at your present workplace, you will need to avoid using scare words like "ESP." Say instead, "My first hunch is . . ." or, "Has anyone thought of trying such-and-such?" Then quickly back up your intuition with appropriate research. Intuition by any other name will sound like brilliant business sense.

In such a corporation, a man may need to use the same subterfuge. *Intuition* and *sensitivity* have never had a very *macho* ring to them. This sort of stereotyping is as senseless and as insidious as anything that women have to endure. If you're a creative, intuitive man in a do-it-by-the-book company, you may decide to keep your ESP training to yourself and a few like-minded friends, while at the same time strengthening your resolve with affirmations such as the following:

I am becoming more intuitive every day.
I have a secret weapon to help me in my work.
I am a psychic pioneer.
I am transforming the company through ESP.
I can do anything.
I am here for the fun of it.
This is all a game the inner child is playing.

In the American workplace, sex roles and corporate roles still have a way of overlapping. This is one reason that some men find it difficult working for a woman boss. If you're a man who finds himself answering to a woman and not liking it, you need to remind yourself that it's not a *woman* who's telling you what to do, but a talented person in a particular corporate role who is telling you what to do. You've got to get over seeing male and female, and see instead energies, capabilities, and human beings.

If you don't care for some of the directives your female boss has been issuing, do a relaxation exercise and go into a meditation. In that "truth zone," ask your inner self what is really happening here. Are the boss's orders bad ones, or is the problem simply that a woman is telling you what to do? If it's the latter, offer yourself forgiveness and encouragement, recognizing that it's not easy to get over ingrained cultural attitudes in a moment.

Again, affirmations can help. If you really have decided you want to change your attitude toward your female boss, repeat the following:

Women executives are just what this company needs.
Women bring valuable and unique experiences to bear on
  corporate problems.
Women have an intuitive edge that can help us all.
Men and women need the perceptions that the other can
  supply.
Women are my allies.
Together, we can transform this company.

If more men would permit themselves such affirmations, the corporate world would soon be a more humane place. In the meantime, women must carry on their own struggle. If you're a woman who finds that some male executives leave you out of business-related activities, don't accept that situation, but at the same time don't take it personally. Many men are still

197

afraid of women, partly, one suspects, because they are afraid of the feminine side of themselves. Such men have a tendency to categorize women by role—mom, mistress, daughter, wife, secretary—and none of those people seems to belong in the boardroom. Men with this attitude don't know what to make of a woman who is their equal in rank, intelligence, and drive, and so they avoid the issue by circumventing women whenever possible.

Instead of becoming angry, women may find it helpful to allow themselves a touch of reverse sexism, at least in the privacy of their own thoughts. As an exercise, tell yourself, "The poor guys! They mean well, but they don't know the first thing about women and how to be with them. I'll have to help them." Such an approach recognizes that their defensive behavior is their problem, not yours, and that by excluding you they are losing out on some extremely valuable input.

And then just play with them, not in the role of employee or of vice president of sales, or whatever label you labor under, but in the special way that a confident, witty woman can play with a man. No, I'm not talking about flirtation here. Instead, I'm suggesting that you invite their inner child to come out and play. Little girls can be pretty mean stickball players! Even crusty old businessmen tend to respond to the approach of the inner child. Show them you can be a fun friend, not just a fainting female flower, and you may soon find yourself getting invited along on those golf games with the board chairman.

It might help, too, if you were actually good at golf (or poker, or whatever adult version of stickball is played as the sport of privilege at your company). One of the reasons women are not invited along, or not invited a second time, is that they're not thought to be very good at many traditionally male games or sports. If you do, in fact, despise the idea of knocking a little white ball around a great big field all day, then don't waste your time wangling an invitation to go. But more and more, these days, women are involved in sports of all kinds, from aerobics to body-building. Many women can swap Dave Winfield statistics with the most sports-minded of the men. If you happen to be one such woman, don't hide the fact.

If you're not, it might be worthwhile to do a relaxation exercise and then to make meditative contact with your inner self. Ask that self what you are comfortable with, and what you want out of your career anyway. Your child-self is certainly not in it for the job title or for stress or for moral compromise. She is in it for the joy, of it. She is in it to play her game. If playing the company's game (whether the game be golf or office politics) is distressing to the child, it may not be worth the aggravation.

If you like men, have an affinity (or at least an extensive tolerance) for sports, and want to have a free, comradely office relationship with your male colleagues, that's fine. But you should also understand that the more comfortable men are, the more likely they are to behave like—men. Don't go out for beers with them after work and then be shocked if one of them tells an off-color joke. The men are probably not harassing you but complimenting you, by treating you as an equal—one of the boys. It all depends on your own temperament. I know a couple of women stockbrokers who, when they get to "dishing," would make a sailor blush.

Not all the men in the office are mired in sexist attitudes. Find the enlightened, progressive ones and make allies of them. Allow them to even champion you—but discreetly, because this is a delicate area. It must not seem that the chivalrous men are protecting and promoting the defenseless woman of the office. That can backfire very quickly and in the end reinforce the sexual typecasting you're trying to overcome. What all this means, really, is that you have to be subtle and a bit Machiavellian to succeed in some corporate environments. Learn how to use people to your and their own advantage.

The fact is, businesspeople use one another all the time. It's called networking. In decades past, it was the "old boy network"; but nowadays women do it, too. Women executives can give other women a boost up, a prestigious assignment, a break. The way to succeed is to make alliances, not enemies. Find a protector, male or female, who believes in you, and let that person help. It is not always understood that people are pleased and gratified when they feel they are helping a protégée, particularly if that protégée is talented, personable, and bright. Who wouldn't want to be able to say that he helped out Kay Koplovitz (president of the USA Cable Network), or movie mogul Sherry Lansing, or newspaper magnate Katherine Graham, or *Vogue* editor Anna Wintour at an early point in her career?

There are some situations, of course, in which a sponsor-protégée relationship of this kind can backfire and have long-term negative results. One is a situation in which there is the appearance a sexual *quid pro quo*. Sleeping one's way to the top is not only frowned upon; it almost never works. Any woman attempting it will most likely end up with a "fun fur," a ride on a yacht, and, not long thereafter, a pink slip.

A sponsorship can also sour if the protector feels in some way threatened by the protégée. We all like to lend a hand at times, but no one wants to be supplanted.

It doesn't work, either, when there is ingratitude or a take-it-for-granted attitude by the person being helped. Such errors in judgment can turn a powerful friend into an even more powerful enemy.

One of the most counterproductive situations is that in which women disparage other women instead of helping them. In some corporations, where only so many women are allowed into the executive suite, destructive competition still exists. It gives further life to all the sexist stereotypes of female cattiness, and in the end it harms the careers of those who engage in it. It would be far better for women executives, at whatever level, to work together to open up the corporation so that *all* women can rise to the level of their fullest potential.

Make friends with your women colleagues whenever possible and set up informal get-togethers to talk over common experiences at the office. You definitely need a support group of some kind. You need a free and open exchange of opinions, a pooling of resources, a sharing of contacts. If you are unfortunate enough to be in a company where competition among the women precludes this kind of sharing, contact professional women's groups and get some outside support and advice.

One problem that both men and women have to face is

whether or not to have children—and, if so, how to do it. In the heyday of the feminist movement, women were encouraged to believe that they could have it all. They could go out and have a career and at the same time raise a bunch of lovable and perfect children, all without skipping a beat. It turns out to be only partly true. Having a child is very likely to hold your career back, at least for a while. Let's face it, if your baby has a 104-degree fever and you have a board meeting to attend, you will have to make a choice. It is a choice that more and more dads have to make as well.

Exercise: Should I Have a Child?

This is an exercise for both men and women.

Get yourself into a relaxed state. Visualize a white movie screen before you and count slowly down from ten to one, sinking more deeply into your subconscious with every step.

The following instructions are for women only:

Imagine your child-self, the little sweet-natured sorceress within you. Say hello, feel at home in her presence, then quietly ask her what she thinks about the idea of your having a child. If there is an upward rush of warm feeling about it, that's a positive sign. If you sense a hesitation, a shrinking back, that is important to know.

Now, using your power of creative visualization, look ahead to the birth of the baby. Feel all the pain of childbirth, and ask yourself if you feel it's worth it to go through this. Then see yourself afterward, holding the baby. Are you happy? Is there a man there with you? Will he be helping to change the baby? Does he have a frown on his face? Do you think he will quickly get tired of dealing with a crying child?

Visualize yourself two months after the birth. Are you still at home or back at work? Do you see yourself as happy? Do you see yourself breast-feeding? Do you have help with the baby? Is the man there, or a hired helper? Do you trust these other people? Do you feel you are

201

missing out by not being at the office? If you are at the office, do you feel you've missed out by not being at home with the baby? Think about the corporation for which you work. How flexible is it? Would it be possible to keep your present job, but work one or two days a week at home? How flexible is the man in your life? Visualize him. How will he handle fatherhood? How will you handle motherhood?

The following instructions are for men:

Imagine your child-self. Feel his presence within you, then ask what his real feelings are about your becoming a father. Do the anxieties you experienced in your conscious mind about the increased responsibility and the loss of independence persist on this deeper stratum of consciousness, or do you feel a basic affirmation and excitement?

Now, look ahead. Do you see yourself actively participating in birth preparation classes and assisting in the delivery room? Can you see yourself later changing diapers, getting up in the middle of the night, hurrying home after work? When you were growing up, what was your own father's role in taking care of the children? Do you identify with his approach or reject it?

Actually, if you have trouble picturing yourself as "Mr. Mom," up to your elbows in soiled diapers, that doesn't mean you should avoid parenthood. There are many aspects of the experience that you cannot imagine until you are dealing with them. The important things to find within yourself are a basic acceptance of the idea of fatherhood and a commitment to following through on the responsibilities that come with it.

FEMININITY IN THE CORPORATE WORLD

Many women feel a conflict at times between their femininity and the corporate role they have elected to play. They ask themselves if it's possible to nail down tough business deals every day without in the process sacrificing their soft, nurturing sides. That's a tough question, in fact one of the central man/woman questions in this time of radical social transition. The short answer is, yes, you can do it. But as always, meditation can help. It is in the subconscious, on the ground floor of your being, that the issue must be resolved. Follow up your meditation with affirmations about femininity and power, perhaps including the following:

Sensitivity is powerful.
Powerful women are sexy.
My emotional vulnerability is a strength.
A strong, competent woman is attractive to strong men.
My intelligence attracts intelligent men.
I accept and celebrate my complexity.

Our assumptions about appropriate male and female behavior are constantly being challenged by the shifting demands of our lives. Women now constitute over 46 percent of the work force, and very few of them view working as a way to keep busy between meetings of the bridge club. Increasingly, and by necessity, we live in a two-paycheck society.

Men have begun to accept this new reality. What has come as a bit of a shock to them, however, is that more and more working women are not satisfied with merely having a job. They want a career—even a demanding, high-powered career. They want the same prerogatives that men have long sought for themselves.

But they still want to be attractive to men. That can be a problem if the men they want to attract are threatened by decisive, successful women. It can be a problem if the men need to be the boss, or if they think a woman's place is in the home.

Keep in mind, however, that you generally get what you ask for. If you are having major problems with men who cannot accept your career successes, maybe on some level you have been asking for that trouble in your life, because you haven't accepted your own success. If you have mixed feelings about that, you are probably sending out mixed messages.

Again, affirmations can be a great help. Let yourself know, a number of times each day:

I deserve all my successes.
I am a fine and rare human being.
I am made for happiness.
I deserve a happy and mutually supportive love relationship.
I attract people who love and accept me just as I am.

Once you have aligned yourself with the clear and positive energy within yourself, you will find much less confusion in your romantic liaisons. You will no longer be asking for conflict, but for confluence, a meeting of open, generous minds.

As a rule, though, it is best to keep all romantic liaisons out of the workplace. If you're involved with someone you work with, I would suggest trying to compartmentalize your life, so that you can deal with your lover strictly as a business associate during business hours. Not everyone can do this, and the results can be disastrous at raise or promotion time, particularly if your lover is a subordinate and you're the one who decides who's getting the raises. Even if you are corporate equals, it is hard to give your full attention to work when the object of your emotional confusion strides past your office. It's hard enough to keep the social and sexual equations in balance at work without creating additional confusion.

It's better to keep the emotional messages clear and non-passionate in the workplace. There are some corporate types, of course, who don't get the right message because they are listening to their own little demons. That's when you may find yourself facing the most uncomfortable and demeaning of office problems, that of sexual harassment.

This particular affliction comes in many forms, and it may

last a day, a year, or a lifetime. A 1988 government report said that an astounding 42 percent of the women who work for the federal government say they've been sexually harassed in the last two years. Sexual harassment is defined by the Equal Employment Opportunity Commission as "unwelcome or unsolicited verbal, physical, or sexual conduct that is made a term or condition of employment, is used as the basis for employment or advancement decisions, or has the effect of unreasonably interfering with work or creating an intimidating, hostile or offensive work environment."

Such harassment can be very tricky for a woman to handle. First of all, it's not always easy to be sure it's really harassment and not just office banter. Maybe in some cases it's even a clumsy form of wooing. Who knows, this annoying character may be a good-hearted guy who just doesn't know how to approach you.

As if things weren't confusing enough, there's now a growing phenomenon called corporate kissing. Perhaps because there are more and more women in the work force, the peck on the cheek between businesspeople has become almost as common as the handshake, and a lot more confusing for both sexes. Even *The Wall Street Journal* (July 6, 1988) has taken notice of it, asseverating that "etiquette gurus say corporate kissing is usually a *faux pas* unless the participants are close friends outside the workplace."

And then there's the corporate hug. Continues the *Journal:* "Women may be more likely to initiate a corporate kiss, but the corporate hug usually starts with a man." Such hugs are frequently bestowed on "female colleagues or subordinates. And the hugs can be abusive."

Although abusiveness used to be almost exclusively a male phenomenon, women today may also be guilty of using physical contact in a way that makes their male colleagues (subordinates and superiors) uncomfortable. Women may behave in ways that have sexual or nurturing overtones that are resented by their coworkers. Often these "endearments" are not intended to be abusive, but they may feel that way to the recipient.

205

An acquaintance of mine ended up quitting his job at a major cosmetics firm because of extracurricular demands made on him by his female boss. It happened that those demands were social rather than sexual: she made him serve as her escort to frequent social affairs and led him to understand that if he refused he should not expect a raise. It may be important, then, for men as well as women to participate in the following exercise.

Exercise: The Psychic Shield

In order to discover what is really going on, it is useful to do a meditation. In a quiet, private place, go through the exercise, "Making Contact," outlined in Chapter Two. When you feel in touch with your subconscious, ask about the person who's been annoying you. You should get some clear images and feelings. If you get a sense of threat, or see a shadow moving toward you, you pretty much have your answer.

Then ask about yourself. Is it possible you are sending out signals that you are not aware of? This is never an excuse for sexist behavior, but the meditation exercise will tell you if you have in some way been inviting sexual reactions. If you haven't been, if you dress and act professionally at all times, then you do need to find a way to protect yourself from the rogue male or predatory female in the office.

While still in that quiet, inward state, create a psychic shield for yourself. Visualize, as concretely as you can, a mirror all around you, facing out. Imagine all the aggressive sexual energy being directed at you suddenly being reflected back at the sender. It's a little like the old childhood rejoinder: "I'm rubber, you're glue. Everything you say bounces off me and sticks to you!"

Why should this work? It may sound too simple to be effective. But we are all surrounded by a force field, and these fields of psychic energy interact, attracting what they are magnetized toward, repelling what they're magnetically opposed to. There may be a touch of psychic suggestion in this, too. Hypnotists have used it for centuries. For instance, you may be told, while under hypnosis, that a bowl of cold water is really boiling hot. If you then hold your fingers in the water, you will eventually get burn blisters. The left side of your brain may say, "How is this possible?" The right side replies, "Don't worry about it; it's magic."

So each morning before you leave for work, put up your psychic mirrors, your personal invisible shield, your attitude of invulnerability. Remember, you don't *have* to react to sexual innuendoes and smarmy jokes. In fact, since part of your tormentor's purpose is to get a rise out of you, nonreaction can frequently be an effective deterrent.

If nothing seems to work and the abuse continues, you may have to take further action. If the abuser is a man, determine whether he has been bothering other female workers and discuss the harassment with them. Then all of you go to his office and confront him. In calm, determined tones (fury would be counterproductive here), let him know that you are all giving him a chance to change his behavior. One chance. He will probably be so shocked at being confronted in this way that he'll change his office behavior very quickly.

However, if he doesn't, then go directly to the man's superior. Either alone or with your delegation of women, tell him calmly what has been going on. Say that none of you desires to go to court with a sexual harassment case, and that you're sure the problem can be taken care of at the present management level.

It would be extremely unusual if that did not do the trick. Still, there are instances when nothing seems to work, when a whole department is permeated with an attitude of sexual aggression. For five years, Catherine Broderick worked as an enforcement attorney at the Washington regional office of the Securities and Exchange Commission. In an interview in *The Washington Post,* she claims that the office managers "created their own little world . . . Each one had to have his own girlfriend or mistress in the office, as if it was a competition. They expected you to come in and drop your integrity at the door." After she complained, she says she was given low performance evaluations, was denied promotions, and was threatened with firing.

207

She sued, and for the next nine years she practically impoverished herself with lawyers' fees and other expenses. At last, in May, 1988, a federal judge ruled in her favor. She was awarded back pay plus interest and legal expenses.

It's hard to say if it was worth it. Broderick had to enter therapy to work through her anger, and she still is trying to get to the point where her colleagues view her as an attorney and not as a paranoid complainer. And yet, because of her victory, it may be easier for future women attorneys to work in the SEC without fear of harassment. You might say it was worth it for her successors, but not, certainly, for her own career.

Many people assume that sexual harassment comes about as a reaction to a person's appearance. Most often it does not. Some women, in an effort to avoid being targeted for harassment, dress ultraconservatively, even dowdily, concealing and downplaying their bodies. This is understandable, but unfortunate. Why shouldn't you be yourself?

The goal is to strike a sensitive balance in all aspects of your corporate life. That can be tricky to manage, but it is essential. Be a good listener but not a doormat. Project physical attractiveness without sending out sexual signals. Be decisive and authoritative without crushing the fragile egos of your colleagues. Steer past the rocks of sexual harassment while avoiding the shoals of frumpiness. Don't dress up and don't dress down, and yet look distinctive. The bottom line is: Be yourself.

20 Sharing Prosperity

In May, 1978, two friends named Ben Cohen and Jerry Greenfield opened an ice-cream parlor in a renovated gas station in Vermont. Last year, their company, Ben and Jerry's Homemade, boasted sales of some $45 million, with profits of over $1.5 million. Theirs has been a wild and in fact unintended success, and they've made a point of sharing that success with those who work for them.

Believing that most corporate executives are overpaid, Ben and Jerry came up with the "five-to-one rule" which limits the top salary to five times what the lowest paid worker makes. In 1988, according to research published by Erik Larson in *Inc.* magazine, that meant no one made over $84,240 a year. Top people could make more, of course, as long as they first raised the salaries of those at the bottom.

The company's sensitivity to its workers has not ended there. When Ben and Jerry's went public, shares were first offered only in Vermont, and at a low price, so that workers and neighboring communities could get a jump on owning part of the operation. The company has also set up a foundation which spends 7.5 percent of the company's pre-tax income on social causes. Handicapped people are hired, free therapy sessions are provided for any employee who needs it, and—a small but telling detail—there are changing tables for babies in the men's room as well as in the women's room.

Once a month, production stops so that every employee can attend the staff meeting in the receiving bay of the plant. Here everyone's opinions are sought on company problems, in an effort to replace segmentation with integration. As Rosabeth Moss Kanter argues in *The Change Masters,* such integration is possible when "work is done in an environment of mutual respect, participating teams, multiple ties, and relationships that crisscross the organizational chart." Ben and Jerry's is not perfect, and sometimes communications do get fouled up (employees learned about the company's new Springfield, Vermont, plant, for instance, by reading about it in the newspapers). But the aim of organizational integration remains central. At one staff meeting, Jerry Greenfield actually proposed forming a "Joy Committee," charged with coming up with ways of infusing a little more joy into the work routine.

Hardly your average company. And despite some continuing organizational problems, chief operating officer Fred Lager is essentially correct when he asserts that the company's success proves "you can share your prosperity with your employees, rewrite the book on executive salaries, rewrite the book in terms of how a company interacts with the community—and you can still play the game according to the rules of Wall Street."

I applaud this people-oriented approach to business and the implied understanding that a company does well when the people in it do well. More and more companies are realizing that employees who are treated fairly don't need to go out looking for another job. But employees who don't feel like part of a team, or who are meted out a four percent annual raise when the inflation rate is six percent, will soon begin updating their résumés. In the long run, you share your prosperity or you lose it.

Science tells us that the universe is abundant and that matter cannot be destroyed, merely transformed. Matter, in fact, is energy in disguise. In a sense, the same is true of money. The monetary universe is abundant, and money spent turns into something else which sooner or later can be converted back into money. The use of money, then, is an exchange of energy. Money you spend to benefit the lot of employees transforms itself into better morale, which leads to greater productivity, which results in greater profits. Profit-sharing plans tend to work the same way. Workers who are offered stock in the company become motivated to work harder, because really they are working for themselves. You always get back what you send out.

This doesn't mean throwing money at your people. Rosabeth Moss Kanter makes a good point when she argues, in *The Change Masters,* that "companies need to be encouraged to *invest* in people rather than paying them off—that is, to channel more of their 'rewards' into budgets for projects or new ventures and less into after-the-fact bonuses for executives." That's how you arouse the interest of the creative and ever-curious child-self within you. Offer a challenge and the financial backing to pursue it, and the intuitive part of you will respond with insights and innovations.

But many executives, having made their way up through traditional organizations, cling to a theory of lack rather than of abundance. They're comfortable with the closed, segmental business practices of the past and fearful of the innovative, integrative approaches of the future. They suffer from what I term "Midas-itis." Whatever they touch may turn to gold, but they can't transform that gold into human assets such as loyalty and higher morale because they don't know how to let go of their wealth, and they don't grasp the point that a more open attitude toward money would soon result in still more money.

Boys used to catch monkeys that way in India. A few nuts would be put in a bottle and left overnight. The monkey would come by, thrust in its hand for the nuts, then find it couldn't get its hand out the narrow neck of the bottle—unless, of course, it let go of the nuts. This it could not bring itself to do, and so come morning there it was, trapped by its own greed.

It's shakeout time in America, and the sun is coming up on a landscape littered with the shells of tightfisted companies that tried to maximize short-term profits and withhold prosperity

211

from their workers. Soon, there was no prosperity to withhold.

Such business tragedies may ultimately stem from the way people have been raised. Many budding executives learned early to equate money with power and self-worth. One person I know had to earn quarters shining shoes at a country club when he was young. Later in life, it became his obsession to own that country club. That seemed the best way to overcome those early feelings of powerlessness. Money, for such people, carries an extra emotional buzz that is not warranted. Making and holding onto it becomes an obsession, not a creative game. Such people need a financial methadone program.

You don't have to be deprived to feel deprived. A woman recently came to me for a psychic counseling session. She was in a panic. "I'm down to my last three million dollars," she said. "What should I do?" To her it was a real problem, because she'd started with forty million. An alarming diminution, to be sure, but still, there are ways to squeak by on three million, or to build it back up to forty. But she had the poverty consciousness.

A conscientious chief executive will tend to take on, even without wanting to, the symbolic role of parent in an extended family. A touch of paternalism, if it is a light touch, does not seem to me a bad thing. A parent, after all, isn't doing his job if he doesn't make sure that his family's needs are met. Whether his style is authoritarian or easygoing, a parent wants his children to be happy, fulfilled, challenged. He wants them to see the dentist, have decent health care. He wants to help them set aside money for the future. He does this because he cares about their well-being, not because some regulatory agency or some union will cause him problems if he doesn't.

At the same time, of course, he doesn't want to practice the kind of heavy-handed paternalism that would rob his employees of their incentive. He doesn't want to run a household in which the kids are afraid to speak up, or in which the bearer of bad news gets punished. It is important that all members of the household have a say in household decisions and that he accord them the respect of taking their suggestions seriously.

Such parental precepts seem painfully obvious. Why is it they are so seldom applied to corporate relations?

Exercise: Putting Yourself in the Workers' Shoes

A creative visualization exercise can help to sensitize you to the real needs of your workers. Afterward, do a visualization concerning the profit needs of the company. Then compare those needs and identify the areas in which they seem in accord, as well as the areas in which they seem in conflict.

Yes, there's a touch of King Lear's advice in this exercise. "Take physick, pomp," he cried,

Expose thyself to feel what wretches feel,
That thou may'st shake the superflux to them,
And show the heavens more just.

Your employees are presumably in better fettle than the "wretches" that wrung Lear's heart. But with the fantastic improvement in workers' living conditions in the past several centuries has come an equal rise in expectations. Your people want what you want—a sense of dignity on the job, a salary they can live on, and a feeling that they're moving ahead.

To determine whether these conditions exist, first gather all the information you can about the employees in your immediate jurisdiction. Talk with them, look at their performance records. Then sit back, put yourself into a relaxed condition, and think about one of the people to whom you've been thinking of giving a raise.

See that person clearly in your mind as if on a movie screen. Now, see yourself *as* that person, looking out of that person's eyes at you, the boss, there in your chair. What kind of boss does that person see?

Does he see someone he can talk to honestly? Does he see an antagonist? An unapproachable VIP? A friend?

Still looking out from that employee's eyes, imagine what his or her life is really like. What kind of stress does his particular job entail? Is it incredibly repetitious? Does he get headaches every day from staring at a VDT? Does he live an hour or more away from the office? What is the commute like? Does he have a new child? How is he juggling job and family? Is

213

he able to keep the stresses of his personal life from affecting his job performance?

What kind of reward would be most appropriate? What would increase his incentive to do an even better job in the future? A raise is always in good taste. How much of one?

Or would some other form of recognition—a bonus, a few days' extra vacation time, an award, a corner office—be more suited to his personality and needs?

Where does *he* want to go in his career? Would a promotion help him or divert him from his goal? A promotion to what?

Or would the best reward of all be a commitment from you, backed up with R&D money from the company, to let him pursue a special research project he's been talking up? Would it make the most sense, in other words, to place a bet on his future performance, rather than to reward his past performance?

On some level, we are all accountable for what we do with our prosperity. The more psychic you become, the more keenly you will sense that we are all made up of the same energy and are sustained by the same vibrant energy field. If one part of the field is hurting, the other parts are subtly trembling. That's the ultimate rationale behind the injunction: Do unto others as you would have them do unto you. Because you are doing it unto yourself all the time.

It is easy to dispute this by pointing to certain notorious billionaires who seem to have made their way to the top by pushing others aside. But I think there are far more people who have become wealthy through their ability to bring people together and to create mutually advantageous deals.

And what about those few obnoxious billionaires who've hurt others and triumphed? I don't believe they've triumphed. In all my years of counseling businesspeople, I have yet to meet anyone who has found happiness by selling his soul. Such people stifle their inner child, their lives are likely to be loveless, and their consciences do not bear examination.

How different the lives of those who have attuned their

business goals to humanistic life goals, who are happy to be able to provide employment and to share the prosperity. Once you realize that everyone is connected on the level of psychic energy, business becomes more of a game than ever, because life is more of a pleasure. Ask Ben and Jerry, whose business philosophy emphasizes "fun, charity, and goodwill toward fellow workers up and down the line."

Maybe you'll even start your own "Joy Committee."

21 Where Do We Go from Here?

As you must realize by now, this is a book about power. The techniques presented in the preceding chapters are all, in one way or another, concerned with ways to tap your inner power and to wield your outer power. The implicit message is that human beings are a lot more powerful than they think.

For many, that is a scary message. One reason people may find it so is that the flip side of power is responsibility. It's easier to be a victim, to be a poor player with a losing script written by someone else. What's tough is to accept the fact that you've written your own script and are still writing it. You are ultimately the creator of the conditions in which you find yourself. Where you go from here depends entirely on the decisions you make about the plot you're weaving and the energy with which you throw yourself into your part.

Blame therefore has no meaning to the inner executive. The unreasonable boss, the inept financial advisor, the backstabbing coworker are merely players in the show you're putting on, here on earth. You don't even blame yourself, because you realize there are no mistakes. The more intuitive you become, the more aware you are that even your blunders were self-induced, and that you wouldn't have committed them if you

216

didn't get something out of them. Why have you attracted into your life a surly boss? Why is it that the people you become romantically involved with all happen to be married? What is the subconscious payoff for you in this behavior pattern? When such patterns are no longer useful to you, no longer amusing to your inner scriptwriter, you're ready to write them out of the play.

Another reason people are afraid to acknowledge the extent of their own power is that they link power with oppression and assume that powerful people are bad people. "Power corrupts," they say. What they mean, really, is that power corrupts immature people. Give worldly power to someone who has not developed inner resources and you are soliciting corruption.

As you develop your inner powers, you inevitably begin to change. You become clearer about what you want and what you don't want. You begin to notice certain leadership qualities you didn't know you possessed. But it may be painful at first to manifest those powers in front of those who liked you the way you were. Your family and friends won't want you to change, because they have already long ago decided who you are. It may be disconcerting and a little threatening for them to have to adjust to a different you—particularly to a more independent you. So if you have a strong need for approval, if it is very important for people to like you, the message of this book is going to make you uncomfortable.

The inner executive, after all, is considerate of others, but he does not require their approval. He doesn't need an opinion poll to find out what he thinks. He acts on the authority of his own intuitions.

He is comfortable with power, knowing that its source is within himself. He acknowledges the creator, the god—small "g"—in himself, and looks for it in everyone he meets. It is that spark of truth, of energy, of power that is the source of his happiness. *That's* what it is that distinguishes him from so many of his colleagues: he is actually happy!

His office is his domain, his war room, his intelligence-gathering center. His coworkers are his loyal teammates; even his business adversaries are friendly rivals, rather than en-

217

emies. In fact, although the inner executive is a fierce competitor, he has fewer enemies than anyone else. Those he is competing against are his sparring partners, and the more skillful they are the better he likes it. Who wants to play tennis with someone he knows he can beat?

Look at the changes in yourself since you began doing the exercises in this book. You have learned ways to combat office stress, ways to relax, ways to sink down and make contact with your subconscious self.

You have begun the process of harnessing that primal self and of harvesting its intuitions. You have learned ways to coax the inner child into playing the business game with you. And you have learned how to make contact with the child in others—even in the gruff old chairman of the board.

You've learned how to give yourself a psychic tune-up, how to sweep your aura, how to use colors and other means to turn your office into a meditation chamber without sacrificing its sharp-edged executive look.

You have learned the all-important technique of creative visualization, as well as ways of replacing negative conditionings with positive ones. You've practiced setting goals, and you've learned techniques for product innovation, dream imaging, and the use of the pendulum.

You've begun applying your increasing psychic abilities to issues of the workplace, such as morale, promotions, and sexual harrassment; and you've considered ways to share your increasing prosperity with those who work for you.

Where do you go from here? Go right on developing your intuitive powers, doing and redoing the exercises, finding your psychic strengths and weaknesses. Some people find they are better at one psychic technique than another. Others find that the best method is a combination of methods. In any case, psychic development is not something you do only once. It requires daily practice, somewhat like the discipline required to learn to play the violin. Even then, of course, not everyone will become a Heifitz; but most people will at least be able to carry the tune that their inner self has been singing all their life. At the same time, they will be sharpening their competitive edge in business.

218

Most investments take time before they become profitable. Your investment of time and effort in yourself, if you have the "stick-to-itiveness" needed to see it through, will bring you long-term profits of many kinds. Besides the financial rewards, the investment helps create the four conditions without which success has no meaning:

1. You find that you like your work more than you ever thought you would.

2. Your health is much better than in the past, since stress has been reduced and destructive behavior patterns reversed.

3. Your love relationships grow deeper, more satisfying, yet at the same time less predictable. They almost have to, as you become more sensitive and psychically energized. People are aware of your greater openness and feel drawn to you, knowing you do not take them for granted.

4. You discover the happiness—in fact, relief—of expressing yourself, rather than repressing yourself. This means more than speaking up at a meeting; it means fully engaging with the world in open psychic dialogue. Your feelings about things are not calcified opinions from the past, but bright, sudden revelations from your intuitive self. They surprise you as much as they surprise your listeners.

As you become more adept at accessing your ESP, your attitude toward business changes. If your job once seemed like drudgery, it has now become a game, one you wish everyone could learn to enjoy playing. Too many of your peers seem to be clawing their way grimly to the top, their hearts weighed down by obligation, their health endangered by stress, their integrity compromised by corner-cutting, expense-padding, and other shortsighted ploys for getting ahead. There is nothing sadder, in a way, than the spectacle of those executives at the Beech-Nut Corporation who in 1988 were found guilty of conspiring to sell bottles labled "pure apple juice," although they contained no apple juice at all. The executives saved millions of dollars for their company (presumably furthering their own careers in the process) by the simple expedient of taking food from the mouths of babies.

The inner executive, aware as he is of the invisible, infinitely responsive energy field just beneath the surface of events, would see that such a scheme was doomed from the start. Even if it had outwardly "succeeded," it was doomed, because whatever energies a person sends out, the same eventually return to him. Indeed, he attracts them, just as an angry person draws an angry response from others. Call it the ancient idea of karma, or call it the new physics; the truth is, we are all bound up in a self-woven net of causes and effects. Some of the results of our actions may take many years to work their way out into the world of indictments and other externalities; but other effects we feel immediately. For instance, not wanting to look at ourselves in the mirror. For instance, no longer having access to the intuitive, joyful part of ourselves. Any business triumph arrived at by immoral means is at best a Pyrrhic victory. It is a success that tastes like disaster.

Exercise: Writing Your Obit

This is somewhat similar to the exercise, "Visualizing Your Life Backwards," in Chapter Seventeen. But whereas the point of that exercise was to devise ways to rise in the company, the object of this one is to discover how you want to be remembered.

Robert Moses, who was neither engineer nor architect, is remembered as "the master builder" for his ability to make things happen in New York City. The force of his vision and the power of his personality were the only "power tools" he needed to bulldoze the slums and create Lincoln Center, the West Side Highway, and the United Nations building, among other projects. Chiseling your image in the New York City skyline is certainly one way to be sure you are remembered, but it's not everyone's style. Sister Teresa has used quite a different set of power tools, plugged into the greatest power source of all; and her most grandiose building projects have to do with the construction of new shelters for beggars and new hospices for lepers.

You have your own vision of your life and what it stands for, although you may never have sat down and tried to put that vision into words.

Now would be a good time to do that. Take a pad and fill a page or two with notes for your own obituary. Write it in newspaper style, and feel free to fulfill your deepest dreams, even fantasizing a bit about the occasion and date of your demise. For instance: "Brimley Shortchange, famed industrialist and explorer, died yesterday when his parachute failed to open during an air show outside of Paris. He was eighty-two."

Then, in paragraph two, get down to what you were mainly known for, what innovations you introduced into the business world, and how you were regarded by your colleagues. This is a fantasy projection, but it has a serious purpose and it should grow out of your true sense of who you are. Don't claim any accomplishments that you don't think you are going to be able to bring off.

Do you read in this imaginary obituary that you were happily married? That you had children and grandchildren? Or did you die single at age 36 of a bleeding ulcer on the floor of the Stock Exchange while yelling out a bid?

Are the workers in your company in shock over the loss of their beloved and benevolent employer, or are they jumping up and down and singing, "Ding, dong, the wicked witch is dead"?

Finally, after drafting your obit, take a careful look at its tone. Is it triumphant or wistful? Are there accomplishments you would have liked to put down but didn't feel you could?

Now, on a separate page, make a wish list of your life's accomplishments—even the wildest and least "realistic." If these are truly things you need to do during this life, maybe they're not so unrealistic after all. Try visualizing them actually taking place. If you can see them, vividly and in detail, then you can do them. Tell yourself: "Whatever I can conceive, I can achieve."

Now go back and revise the obituary, adding these projects to the list. And make a private vow to yourself that you will carry out every one of them.

This book has emphasized the liberated feeling that comes from viewing business as a game. Your relaxed enjoyment of

221

your job is an implicit statement of a corporate credo. You tend to rise easily through the ranks because you don't put mental roadblocks in your path. You're almost maddeningly cheerful during tense negotiations. You laugh all the way to the bank.

But there are many levels to the game, and business can be more than a jolly round of Monopoly. It can be a creative act, in the sense that writing a novel or a symphony are creative acts. Once the creator in you is engaged, it hardly matters what enterprise it is engaged in. The act of creation is the same.

On that level, business transcends its own processes and becomes a metaphor for life. Just as you are the creator of the business you want to run, you are cocreator with the universe of the life you want to live. The more intuitive you become, the more you realize that business, like life generally, can be a cooperative enterprise. It's not necessary for someone else to lose in order for you to win. In fact, the way to win is to share your prosperity, to help those around you, and to convert adversaries into allies.

The numerous techniques presented in this book, then, do not represent ingredients in a recipe for success; they represent propositions in a philosophy of life. Followed diligently, they actually change your whole psychic polarity, aligning you with the generative forces of the universe.

When you go into the business world with that kind of advantage, you are bound to achieve remarkable things.

22 Your ESP IQ: Second Quiz

They say that one reason chess is such an unusual game is that you can know all the rules to it and still not really know how to play it. Learning to play takes a lifetime. The same can be said of ESP training. Now that you've read this book and tried out the techniques, you "know the rules." And they aren't such complicated rules, really. But proficiency increases gradually, with frequent practice, over a period of months and years.

The basic techniques we've discussed—especially meditation, dream imaging, use of the pendulum, and creative visualization—comprise what I call the psychic tool kit. These tools are most effective when kept well-oiled, well-sharpened, and in frequent use. You may start out by building a simple clubhouse for your inner child to play in; you may end up building an empire.

The purpose of this follow-up ESP quiz is to see how well you've learned to use these tools so far. Don't expect to get all the answers right; this is a book on intuition, not on omniscience. Any accuracy rate better than, say, twenty-five percent for the Meditation Quiz and Dream Quiz or fifty-five percent for the Pendulum Quiz suggests that you are receiving input from the psychic side of your personality. That intuitive edge will only increase as you continue to practice.

Many people find that they get better results with one technique than with another. That's fine. It just means that the subconscious is more engaged with one "game" than with the others. In general, I say go with your strengths and rely on the methods that have proven most reliable; but at the same time continue practicing the other techniques, because powers tend to develop the more you concentrate on them.

Meditation Quiz

Use the meditation techniques you've been practicing (as outlined in Chapter Two) to quiet down the noise of the conscious mind and to sink into yourself until you "touch bottom" on the subconscious level. This state, as we've mentioned, is neither sleep nor hypnosis, but a kind of waking, self-controlled "trance" during which certain pictures arise spontaneously before the mind's eye. It's a subtle thing, a matter of the subtlest hints and impulses. Don't expect yourself to be transported into Walt Disney's *Song of the South*. It's much more similar to the state that poets, composers, and other artists get "lost" in when they're in the midst of image-making free association. These pictures may or may not constitute "answers" to the questions you ask. Often the images have only an oblique relationship to the problem at hand and will need some interpreting.

Have before you a fresh pad and pen and be ready to jot down whatever word or image comes to mind in response to each question. The ideal arrangement would be to have a friend read you the questions—but no conversation about them until you've finished.

Once you feel yourself in the meditative state, visualize a "psychic TV screen" and allow images to appear there in response to the following questions:

1. You are planning to buy some stock in a computer company, but you can't decide among IBM, Apple, Compac,

Epson, or Hewlett-Packard. Which of these computer stocks will perform best over the next month?

2. Which television network will win the ratings race this coming month? What will the ratings picture look like for all three networks?

3. What segment of your company's business will improve the most during the next month?

4. What actor will appear in next month's biggest movie hit?

5. What companies will be involved in the next takeover bid that you learn about?

6. What is going to happen to the mutual funds market in the next thirty days?

7. Think about someone you are very close to. What will be the biggest change, or most exciting event, in that person's life over the next thirty days?

8. What do you think will be the most memorable thing that happens to you during that same time-period?

9. What will the unemployment picture be in the United States a month from now? Will unemployment levels rise or fall?

10. What will be the big news out of the Middle East during the next thirty days?

You'll have the answers to all these questions within the next month. Some answers can be obtained by placing a call or two to brokers or analysts, others by reading the papers.

Pendulum Quiz

To test properly your skill in the use of the pendulum, you must ask questions that represent a choice between alternatives. Most frequently, that will be a choice between yes and no. It's essential to be specific, even to the point of being obvious; include geographical considerations and the time-frame. As mentioned in Chapter Thirteen, it doesn't matter particularly what material your pendulum is made of, or what its shape is, but it should be something with which you feel a personal connection. Face north and ask each question with great concentration. As we've explained earlier, an up and down motion by the pendulum indicates yes; a back-and-forth motion indicates no.

1. In the next thirty days, will I find a new way to increase my family's income?

2. Will the price of gold in the U.S. change by more than ten dollars per ounce during that time?

3. Will the direction of that change in U.S. gold prices be downward during the next month?

4. Will I be making an unexpected trip during the coming month?

5. How about housing starts in my part of the country? Will they be up overall during the next thirty days?

6. Will inflation rise in the U.S. during the next month?

7. Will mortgage rates rise in the U.S. during the next month?

8. Will our company's gross sales increase during the next thirty days?

9. Will I come down with any illness during the next thirty days?

10. Over the next four weeks, will our company receive some major publicity in the local media?

Dream Quiz

The results of this exercise are a little tricky to tabulate. Not only can you ask yourself just one question per night, but the answers you get from the subconscious may require an interpretation. For a real personal or business problem, it's also a good idea to ask for guidance on several different nights.

First, quickly review Chapter Nine on the procedure, including the "dream notebook" and the bedtime ritual. Then, when you're ready to sleep, ask for dream guidance on one particular question. Ask it three times, with calm concentration, then take a few sips of water and close your eyes.

When you wake up, take another sip or two and remember all you can, jotting down the images and underlying feelings of the dream(s) in your notebook.

First Night. I have a little money now to invest. Over the next month, would I get the best return on this money from stocks, CDs, precious metals, or bonds?

Second Night. Is now the best time for me to put money into real estate in my area, or would conditions be better a month from now?

Third Night. Over the next four weeks, can I expect my company's net profits to rise or to decline?

Fourth Night. I'm thinking of putting some money in grain futures in the next day or two. Thirty days from now, which investment would yield the largest profit—corn, oats, soybeans, or wheat?

Fifth Night. I have some money to invest in industrial futures. Thirty days from now, which investment would do the best—crude oil, heating oil, lumber, or unleaded gasoline?

Sixth Night. How will the dollar be faring a month from today in relation to the other major currencies?

Seventh Night. Will my company's major competitor outperform us in the next month, and if so in what area?

Creative Visualization

There is no quiz for this technique, because it is not about asking questions; it is about projecting realities. You use it to create a result. As we mentioned in Chapter Seven, visualizing does not deny what presently exists, nor is it wishful thinking; it is the creation of self-fulfilling prophecies. It is perhaps the most powerful tool in your psychic tool kit.

Using the techniques explained in Chapter Seven, do a creative visualization on an upcoming event. Choose something that you'll have the results on within a few days or weeks. Then take yourself through that event, step by step, until you arrive at the desired conclusion. Repeat the visualization exercise every day until the event takes place.

The following are some events you might try out your visualization techniques on:

1. You are getting ready to make an important presentation at a sales meeting.

2. You are about to fly off on a business trip.

3. You have an appointment for a job interview at a new company.

4. You are going to meet with the bank's loan officer to discuss your application for a business loan.

5. You are closing on a property and want the meeting to go smoothly.

6. You are about to negotiate the terms of a contract.

7. You are getting ready to go in to see the boss about a raise or promotion.

8. You find you have to fire an employee who's been with the firm a long time.

9. You need to confront a colleague about the quality of his work and the frequency of his absences.

10. You are working up the courage to ask someone to marry you.

After any session using creative visualization, or the pendulum, or the meditation techniques, or dream imaging, remember to reward yourself. Whenever you have a success, however minor it may seem, celebrate that success. The intuitive self is both bold and shy—bold in its flashes of insight, but conditioned to be dominated or ignored by the imperious logical mind. It needs positive reinforcement.

So thank yourself. Take yourself to lunch. Do something for the child part of you, even if it's just going to a movie. With that sort of playful, positive approach, you'll find your ESP moments occurring more frequently, your insights deepening, and your enjoyment of life increasing.

Guide for
the Lazy Executive

If you feel that you don't have the time to spend developing your own ESP abilities, or if you've done the exercises but are reluctant to rely on your own psychic flashes, you may want to consult a professional psychic. Even if you are committed to developing your own abilities, it can be beneficial to double-check your perceptions against those of others.

The problem with finding a reliable psychic is that there are no licensing or regulating procedures governing the field. The Better Business Bureau won't help you. Anyone can call himself a psychic. As a result, there are many frauds, and an equal number of sincere but deluded individuals who simply don't have the goods.

Probably the safest way to find a competent psychic is by word of mouth. Has someone you know and respect had a positive experience using a particular psychic?

Another approach is to talk to the police department in your city or in a neighboring city and ask if they use psychics for solving crimes. (More police departments do so than is generally known.) Ask for their names.

You might also check with certain bookstores, particularly those specializing in ESP and the occult. Such stores are often a clearinghouse for such information. The proprietor has probably heard all the stories, good and bad, about people in your area who do psychic consulting.

And then shop around. Try a few of them out. But when you do, keep the following criteria in mind:

1. If you see a crystal ball in the window, keep walking. A down-at-heel storefront psychic is not likely to be genuine. For one thing, the best psychics are prosperous. Their accuracy has caused people to come back again and again and to recommend their service to others. Many psychics work out of their homes—and very nice homes they are.

2. Go in with an open attitude, neither anxious to believe nor determined to debunk. Ask about the person's references and track record. But don't ask trick questions; they're insulting and any real psychic will see through them. It's better to be frank about what you are doing. Tell him you're aware that many so-called psychics are not what they claim to be and that you'd like to ask some test questions, things he could not possibly know through mere logic. For example, ask him for a profile of your business during the past six months. He should be able to tell you, because that has already happened. If he can't read the past, he can't read the future. Any genuine psychic would take that sort of questioning with good grace.

3. Beware any psychic consultant who asks you questions. A real psychic will sit down with you and very quickly begin telling you things about yourself, your business, your personal life. He won't fish for information from you first.

4. Expect an established flat rate for the reading when you go in. If the rate has escalators—twenty dollars more for advice about additional areas of concern—call a halt right there. The person is probably a phony.

5. Even genuine psychics have areas of specialization. Some are "business psychics," some do best on the subject of personal relationships. Be sure to ask.

6. Psychics may use different tools, or none at all, to do their reading. One may use a pendulum, another may consult a tarot deck, another may work with astrology charts. Some psychics may even go into a trance state. The methods are not important; they are the triggers that set the psychic's intuitive

self in motion. There's only one thing to be concerned about: Are you getting correct information?

7. If you walk away impressed but not convinced, you may want to go back and do another trial run. In any case, think about the experience later, do a meditation on it, perhaps even apply your pendulum to it. Use your intuition, in other words, to decide whether the consultant's intuition is genuine.

PSYCHIC RESOURCE LIST

The following short list is meant to serve as a point of departure for your own investigations. It does not attempt to be exhaustive, or to make claims for the organizations and individuals listed. But each of these sources can provide you with information and referrals to help you find the consultant you need.

Association for Research and Enlightenment
P.O. Box 595
Virginia Beach, VA 23451

The Foundation of Truth
P.O. Box 7133
Atlanta, GA 30309
(404) 875-7846

National Spiritual Science Center of
Washington, D.C.
5605 16th Street, NW
Washington, D.C. 20011
(202) 723-4510

The Quest Bookshop
619 West Main Street
Charlottesville, VA 22901
(804) 295-3377

Spiritual Frontiers Fellowship
10819 Winner Road
Independence, MO 64052

SELECTED BIBLIOGRAPHY

Cerminara, Gina. *Many Mansions*. New York: Signet, 1967.

De Ropp, Robert S. *The Master Game*. New York: Dell, 1968.

Fox, Emmet. *The Sermon on the Mount*. New York: Harper & Row, 1934.

Gawain, Shakti. *Creative Visualization*. San Rafael, CA: Whatever Publishing, 1979. New York: Bantam, 1982.

Goldberg, Philip. *The Intuitive Edge*. Los Angeles: Jeremy P. Tarcher, Inc., 1983.

Grant, Joan. *Winged Pharaoh*. London: William Rider and Sons, 1938.

Hickey, Isabel. *Astrology, a Cosmic Science*. Boston: Fellowship House Bookshop, 1970.

Hill, Napoleon. *Think and Grow Rich*. New York: Fawcett Crest, 1960.

Kanter, Rosabeth Moss. *The Change Masters*. New York: Simon and Schuster, 1983.

Long, Max Freedom. *The Secret Science at Work*. Santa Monica: De Vorss and Company, 1953.

Ostrander, Sheila, and Lynn Schroeder. *Psychic Discoveries Behind the Iron Curtain*. New York: Bantam, 1970.

Rowan, Roy. *The Intuitive Manager*. Boston: Little, Brown, 1986. (New York: Berkley, 1987.)

Siegel, Bernie S., M.D. *Love, Medicine, and Miracles*. New York: Harper and Row, 1986.

Stearn, Jess. *The Power of Alpha-Thinking*. New York: William Morrow, 1976. New York: Signet, 1977.

235

Townley, John. *New Age Career Cycles.* New York: Destiny Books, 1980.

Turkle, Sherry. *The Second Self.* New York: Simon and Schuster, 1984.

Watson, Lyall. *Super Nature.* New York: Bantam, 1974.

Yogananda, Paramahansa. *Autobiography of a Yogi.* Los Angeles: S.R.F. Publishers, 1946.